D1629689

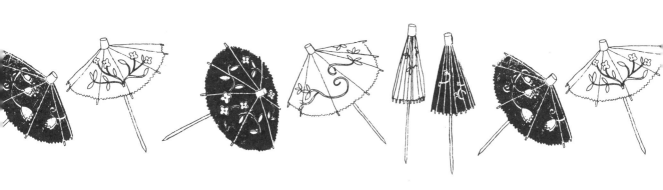

MAKE, SHAKE, COCKTAIL

MAKE, SHAKE, COCKTAIL

DEFINING AND REFINING THE ART OF MIXOLOGY

CONTENTS

This beautiful book, with its delicious recipes and moreish photography, will quickly become an indispensable tool for the budding mixologist. In this comprehensive collection you'll find punches for parties, short drinks for unwinding in the evening and impressive crowd-pleasers for entertaining. All the recipes are simply written to make them easy to follow, and even novice cocktail-makers are guaranteed a winning result every time.

Cocktails have played a colourful part in modern history and have established their place in popular culture. The history of the first cocktail remains a mystery, which has led to a number of entertaining folk tales. One of the more popular stories tells how, during the Revolutionary War, American and French soldiers frequented Betsy's Tavern to enjoy a famous alcoholic concoction of her own creation, known as 'Betsy's Bracer'. One night, amid wild drinking and parties, one of the American soldiers stole a couple of cockerels from a neighbour's garden. He toasted his theft with his drinking companions, saying, 'Here's to the divine liquor which is as delicious to the palate as the cock's tail is beautiful to the eye'. A French officer is said to have responded to the toast with a rousing 'Vive le cocktail!' – and with that, the term cocktail was born!

Since their conception, cocktail trends have come and gone – from the days of the practical cocktail (mixers were used to disguise the sometimes rough flavours of home-made spirits during the Prohibition era in America), to the fancy, frivolous cocktails favoured during the 1980s, and the pared-back, stylish cocktails made famous by stage and screen characters at the turn of the century.

The art of the skilled mixologist is based on a set of easy-to-follow principles that can set almost anyone on the right track to producing an impressive range of cocktails and mixed drinks. This book will give you all the skills you need, and you can apply these to the whole range of cocktail recipes here. Simply read up on the terminology and techniques that follow and get started on the recipes – before long you'll be mixing and shaking with the best of them.

ESSENTIAL EQUIPMENT

COCKTAIL SHAKER

The standard cocktail shaker is a cylindrical metal container with a capacity of 500 ml/18 fl oz. It has a double lid, which incorporates a perforated strainer. If your cocktail shaker doesn't have an integral strainer, you will need a separate one.

MIXING GLASS

This is used for making stirred cocktails. You can use any large container or jug, but you can also buy professional mixing glasses.

STRAINER

A bar or 'Hawthorn' strainer is the perfect tool to prevent ice and other unwanted ingredients being poured from the shaker or mixing glass into the serving glass. If you don't have one, you could use a small nylon strainer instead.

JIGGER OR MEASURE

This small measuring cup is often double-ended and shaped like an hourglass. Standard jiggers are 25 ml and 35 ml, while imperial jiggers are 1 fl oz and 1½ fl oz, representing 1 and 1½ measures respectively. It is the proportions of the various ingredients, not the specific quantities, that are crucial. If you don't have a jigger, you can use the small lid of your cocktail shaker, a shot glass or even a small egg cup.

BAR SPOON

This long-handled spoon is used for stirring cocktails in a mixing glass.

MUDDLER

This miniature masher is used for crushing ingredients, such as herbs and sugar, in the base of a glass. You can also use a mortar and pestle or even the back of a spoon.

OTHER EQUIPMENT

Lots of ordinary kitchen equipment is useful for making cocktails: a corkscrew, a bottle opener, cocktail sticks, a citrus reamer, chopping boards, knives, a citrus zester, a selection of jugs, and a blender for creamy cocktails and slushes. You will also need an ice bucket and ice tongs. Optional extras include swizzle sticks and straws.

MARTINI GLASS

The most immediately recognizable cocktail glass, the Martini glass has a conical shape that helps prevent the ingredients separating, while the stem keeps the drink cool.

COUPETTE GLASS

This glass is based on the earlier champagne coupe, originally used for serving bubbly. The wide bowl is perfect for rimming with salt, making it the ideal glass for serving Margaritas.

HURRICANE GLASS

The shape of this large, short-stemmed glass is said to resemble the hurricane lamp, from which it gets its name. It was originally used for the famous Hurricane cocktail at Pat O'Brien's bar in New Orleans, but today it's more usually associated with exotic frozen and blended cocktails.

CHAMPAGNE FLUTE

The tapered shape of this tall, thin glass is designed to reduce the surface area of the liquid, keeping the champagne bubbly for longer.

HIGHBALL GLASS

Highball glasses are tall and suitable for simple drinks that have a high proportion of mixer to spirit. They are versatile enough to be substituted for the similar, but slightly larger, Collins glass.

LOWBALL GLASS

The terms 'lowball', 'rocks' and 'old-fashioned' are often used to refer to short, squat tumblers. They are perfect for holding ice and are used to serve any spirit 'on the rocks'. They are also useful for short mixed drinks.

SHOT GLASS

A home-bar essential, the shot glass holds just enough liquid to be downed in a single mouthful. Shot glasses have thick bases so that they can withstand being slammed on the bar.

IRISH COFFEE GLASS

The two key features of an Irish coffee glass are heatproof glass and a handle, both of which make it suitable for hot cocktails, such as toddies.

MIXING METHODS

Creating a cocktail is not brain surgery but it does require the deft touch of a skilled mixologist. The better your mixing techniques, the better the quality of the cocktail. Mixing a cocktail is not just a matter of throwing all the ingredients together in a glass, giving them a stir and hoping for the best – there are many different mixing methods, all of which have benefits. The following are the most commonly used methods and the ones that you will find in this book.

SHAKING

This is when you add all the ingredients, with a scoop of ice, to the shaker and then shake vigorously for approximately 5 seconds. The benefit of shaking is that the drink is rapidly mixed, chilled and aerated – after the drink has been shaken, the outside of the shaker will be lightly frosted. Shaking a cocktail also dilutes the drink quite significantly. This dilution is a necessary part of the cocktail-making process and gives shaken recipes the correct balance of taste, strength and temperature.

In addition, shaking can be used to prepare cocktails that include an ingredient, such as egg white, that will not combine effectively with the other ingredients if you use a less vigorous form of mixing.

STIRRING

Once again, you add all the ingredients to a scoop of ice, but this time you combine them in a mixing glass or small jug and then stir the ingredients together using a long-handled bar spoon. As with shaking, this allows you to blend and chill the ingredients without too much erosion of the ice, so you can control the level of dilution and keep it to a minimum. This simple but vital technique is essential for drinks that don't need a lot of dilution, such as a classic Dry Martini.

BUILDING

To 'build' a drink, you simply make it in the glass, in the same way that you make a gin and tonic, for example. It is important to follow the instructions for built cocktails to the letter, as the order of ingredients can change from drink to drink and this can affect the finished flavour.

MUDDLING

Muddling is the term used to describe the extraction of the juice or oils from the pulp or skin of a fruit, herb or spice. A muddler is simply a pestle used to crush the ingredient – you can buy a specific cocktail muddler, or just use the end of a wooden rolling pin.

BLENDING

As the name suggests, this is when the ingredients are combined in a blender! Most blended drinks will have a smooth consistency. The ingredients are usually blended with a scoop of crushed ice and often include items like fresh fruit, which can't be shaken or stirred.

LAYERING

When creating layers in a cocktail you should follow the instructions carefully, putting the heavier spirits or liqueurs into the glass first. If you add them in the wrong order you may find that one layer 'bleeds' into the next, ruining the look of your cocktail.

The first, base layer should be poured into the centre of the glass, without getting any down the sides, if possible. To create the second layer, turn a teaspoon upside down, with the tip touching the inside of the glass, then pour the liquid slowly over the back of the spoon (moving it up the glass as the level rises). Repeat with any remaining liquid ingredients, using a clean teaspoon to pour each new layer.

THE RIGHT ICE

Ice is incredibly important in the world of cocktail mixing. Get it right and you have the basis of an amazing cocktail, get it wrong and it can make a great drink just average.

The ice in a cocktail does two things – during the mixing process it helps to chill and actively mixes the ingredients; once the drink is served it keeps the cocktail cold and prevents too much further dilution. Three types of ice are used in the cocktail recipes here, each with distinctive properties that complement the styles and flavours of the drinks.

CUBED ICE

This is generally used to finish a drink. The more ice you have in your glass, the colder and less diluted your finished cocktail will be. Ice cubes can be made in the freezer in a simple ice tray – 2-cm/¾-inch cubes are the best size for finishing most drinks. The cubes can be broken down and used to make cracked and crushed ice as necessary.

CRACKED ICE

This is smaller than full ice cubes and is generally used in a shaker to chill the liquid ingredients before you strain them. To make cracked ice from whole cubes, simply wrap the cubes in a clean, dry tea towel and give them a gentle knock with a rolling pin. The ice should be broken into pieces no smaller than half a cube.

CRUSHED ICE

This is perfect for blended drinks as it speeds up the mixing process and freezes the whole concoction very rapidly. Crushed or cracked ice is better for some drinks, as you can pack the glass with the maximum amount of ice (cubes leave greater gaps). To make crushed ice, wrap ice cubes in a clean, dry tea towel and knock a few times with a rolling pin. The cubes should be broken into very small pieces.

Many people consider the decoration to be the thing that defines a cocktail. In some cases, your choice of decoration can reflect the ingredients of the drink

FINAL FLOURISHES

itself – think of the Piña Colada with its obligatory pineapple slice. Sometimes the decoration is a vital ingredient but it's usually just added to make the drink look more attractive.

There are basic guidelines for adding the final touches to a drink, but ultimately the way in which you decorate a cocktail will often be down to your imagination and artistic flair.

One of the simplest rules to follow is to match the decoration to the main flavours of the cocktail. Think of your cocktail as a blank canvas – in this book we recommend some simple decorations to go with the recipes, but if you want to have a bit of fun, throw the rule book in the bin and just have a go at creating your own.

Remember – enjoy your drinks, don't make yourself ill and be aware of current government guidelines on alcohol consumption. Experiment to

your heart's content with this book and get the maximum pleasure out of your cocktails by following the recipes, perfecting and using the tried and tested mixing methods and using the right glass for whatever cocktail you are making. Then just decorate and enjoy!

MARTINI

Serves 1

Ingredients

4–6 cracked ice cubes
3 measures gin
1 tsp dry vermouth, or to taste
cocktail olive, to decorate

1. Put the cracked ice cubes into a cocktail shaker.

2. Pour the gin and vermouth over the ice cubes.

3. Shake until well frosted. Strain into a chilled cocktail glass.

4. Decorate with the olive. Serve immediately.

SINGAPORE SLING

Serves 1

Ingredients

cracked ice cubes
2 measures gin
1 measure cherry brandy
1 measure lemon juice
1 tsp grenadine
soda water
lime peel strips and cocktail cherries, to decorate

1. Put 4–6 cracked ice cubes into a cocktail shaker and pour over the gin.

2. Pour over the cherry brandy, lemon juice and grenadine and shake vigorously until well frosted.

3. Half fill a chilled glass with cracked ice cubes and strain over the cocktail.

4. Top up with soda water and decorate with the lime peel and cherries. Serve immediately.

TOM COLLINS

Serves 1

Ingredients

4-6 cracked ice cubes

3 measures gin

2 measures lemon juice

½ measure sugar syrup

soda water

lemon slices, to decorate

1. Put the cracked ice cubes into a cocktail shaker.

2. Pour over the gin, lemon juice and sugar syrup and shake vigorously until well frosted.

3. Strain into a chilled Collins glass.

4. Top up with soda water and decorate with the lemon slices. Serve immediately.

BELLE COLLINS

Serves 1

Ingredients

2 fresh mint sprigs, plus extra to decorate

2 measures gin

1 measure lemon juice

1 tsp sugar syrup

4-6 crushed ice cubes

sparkling water

1. Muddle the mint sprigs.

2. Place the mint in a chilled tumbler and pour in the gin, lemon juice and sugar syrup.

3. Add the crushed ice cubes to the glass.

4. Top up with sparkling water, stir gently and decorate with more fresh mint. Serve immediately.

GIN RICKEY

Serves 2

Ingredients

cracked ice

2 measures gin

1 measure lime juice

soda water

lemon slice, to decorate

1. Fill a chilled highball glass or goblet with cracked ice.

2. Pour over the gin and lime juice.

3. Top up with soda water.

4. Stir gently to mix and decorate with a lemon slice. Serve immediately.

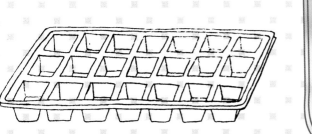

A SLOE KISS

Serves 1

Ingredients

4-6 cracked ice cubes
½ measure sloe gin
½ measure Southern Comfort
1 measure vodka
1 tsp amaretto
splash of Galliano
orange juice
orange peel twist, to decorate

1. Put the cracked ice cubes into a cocktail shaker, pour over the sloe gin, Southern Comfort, vodka and amaretto and shake until well frosted.

2. Strain into a long, chilled glass filled with cracked ice.

3. Splash on the Galliano.

4. Top up with orange juice and decorate with the orange peel. Serve immediately.

1

2

4

SLOW COMFORTABLE SCREW

Serves 1

Ingredients

2 measures sloe gin

orange juice

cracked ice

orange slice, to decorate

1. Shake the sloe gin and orange juice over ice until well frosted and pour into a chilled glass.

2. Dress with a slice of orange and serve immediately.

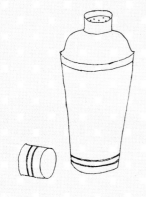

FIREFLY

Serves 1

Ingredients

1 measure gin

½ measure tequila

½ measure dry orange curaçao

½ measure lemon juice

dash egg white

ice

orange peel, to decorate

1. Shake all the liquid ingredients well over ice until frosted.

2. Strain into a chilled cocktail glass and dress with a twist of orange peel. Serve immediately.

GIN SLING

Serves 1

Ingredients

1 sugar cube

1 measure gin

freshly grated nutmeg

lemon slice, to serve

1. Dissolve the sugar in ½ cup hot water in an old-fashioned glass.

2. Stir in the gin, sprinkle with nutmeg, and serve immediately with a slice of lemon.

MAIDEN'S PRAYER

Serves 1

Ingredients

1 measure gin

1 measure triple sec

1 tsp orange juice

1 tsp lemon juice

ice

lemon peel twist,
to decorate

1. Shake the ingredients vigorously over ice until well frosted.

2. Strain into a chilled cocktail glass and dress with the twist of lemon peel. Serve immediately.

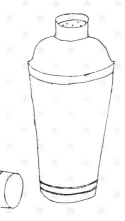

DAISY

Serves 1

Ingredients

4–6 cracked ice cubes
3 measures gin
1 measure lemon juice
1 tbsp grenadine
1 tsp sugar syrup
soda water
orange wedge, to decorate

1. Put the cracked ice cubes into a cocktail shaker.

2. Pour over the gin, lemon juice, grenadine and sugar syrup and shake vigorously until well frosted.

3. Strain the cocktail into a chilled highball glass.

4. Top up with soda water, stir gently and decorate with the orange wedge. Serve immediately.

3

2

4

BLOODHOUND

Serves 1

Ingredients

2 measures gin

1 measure sweet vermouth

1 measure dry vermouth

3 strawberries, plus one to decorate

4–6 cracked ice cubes

1. Put the gin, sweet vermouth, dry vermouth and strawberries into a blender.

2. Add the cracked ice.

3. Blend until smooth.

4. Pour into a chilled cocktail glass and decorate with the remaining strawberry. Serve immediately.

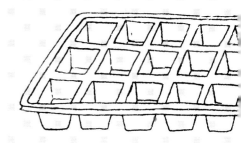

ALASKA

Serves 1

Ingredients

½ measure gin

½ measure yellow Chartreuse

ice cubes

1. Shake the gin and Chartreuse over ice until well frosted.

2. Strain into a chilled glass and serve immediately.

HAWAIIAN ORANGE BLOSSOM

Serves 1

Ingredients

2 measures gin

1 measure triple sec

2 measures orange juice

1 measure pineapple juice

ice

pineapple slices and leaves, to decorate

1. Shake the liquid ingredients vigorously over ice until well frosted.

2. Strain into a chilled wine glass and serve immediately decorated with pineapple slices and leaves.

WEDDING BELLE

Serves 1

Ingredients

2 measures gin

2 measures Dubonnet

1 measure cherry brandy

1 measure orange juice

ice cubes

orange peel, to decorate

1. Shake the liquid ingredients over ice until well frosted.

2. Strain into a chilled glass and serve immediately decorated with a twist of orange peel.

BRIDE'S MOTHER

Serves 1

Ingredients

1½ measures sloe gin

1 measure gin

2½ measures grapefruit juice

½ measure sugar syrup

ice cubes and crushed ice

grapefruit slices, to decorate

1. Shake the liquid ingredients vigorously over ice cubes until well frosted.

2. Strain over crushed ice and dress with grapefruit wedges. Serve immediately.

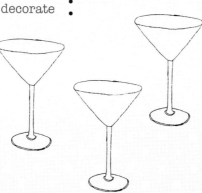

MOONLIGHT

Serves 4

Ingredients

3 measures grapefruit juice

4 measures gin

1 measure kirsch

4 measures white wine

½ tsp lemon zest

ice cubes

1. Shake all the liquid ingredients vigorously over ice until well frosted. Strain into chilled glasses and serve immediately.

Top tip
This light cocktail is ideal to make for several people at once.

SEVENTH HEAVEN

Serves 1

Ingredients

2 measures gin
½ measure maraschino
½ measure grapefruit juice
ice cubes
fresh mint sprigs, to decorate

1. Shake all the liquid ingredients vigorously over ice until well frosted.

2. Strain into a chilled cocktail glass. Dress with fresh mint and serve immediately.

TEARDROP

Serves 1

Ingredients

1 measure gin

2 measures apricot nectar or
peach nectar

1 measure single cream

crushed ice

½ measure strawberry syrup

fresh strawberry and peach
slices, to decorate

1. Put the gin, apricot nectar and cream into a blender and blend for 5–10 seconds until thick and frothy.

2. Pour into a long glass filled with crushed ice.

3. Splash the strawberry syrup on the top and decorate with the strawberry and peach slices. Serve immediately.

BLEU BLEU BLEU

Serves 1

Ingredients

crushed ice

1 measure gin

1 measure vodka

1 measure tequila

1 measure fresh lemon juice

2 dashes egg white

1 measure blue curaçao

soda water

lemon slice, to decorate

1. Put 4–6 crushed ice cubes into a cocktail shaker.

2. Add the gin, vodka, tequila, lemon juice, egg white and curaçao and shake until frosted.

3. Strain the cocktail into a tall glass filled with crushed ice and top up with soda water. Decorate with a lemon slice. Serve immediately.

PINK PUSSYCAT

Serves 1

Ingredients

cracked ice

dash grenadine

2 measures gin

pineapple juice

pineapple slice,
to decorate

1. Half fill a chilled tumbler with cracked ice.

2. Dash the grenadine over the ice and add the gin.

3. Top up with pineapple juice and decorate with
the pineapple slice.
Serve immediately.

BLUE BLOODED

Serves 1

Ingredients

1 measure gin

1 measure passion fruit nectar

4 cubes melon or mango

cracked ice

1-2 tsp blue curaçao

1. Put the gin, passion fruit nectar, melon cubes and
4-6 cracked ice cubes into a blender and blend until
smooth and frosted.

2. Pour into a tall, chilled glass filled with cracked
ice and top with the curacao.
Serve immediately.

GRAND ROYAL CLOVER CLUB

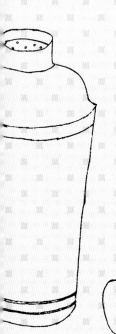

Serves 1

Ingredients

2 measures gin

1 measure lemon juice

1 measure grenadine

1 egg white

ice

lime peel twist, to decorate

1. Pour the first four ingredients over ice.

2. Shake vigorously until well frosted and strain into a chilled cocktail glass.

3. Dress with a twist of lime peel and serve immediately.

Top tip
Cut the lime twist over the finished cocktail to release some of the essence into the drink.

THE BLUE TRAIN

Serves 1

Ingredients

2 measures gin

1 measure triple sec

1 measure lemon juice

splash blue curaçao

cracked ice

1. Pour all of the liquid ingredients into a cocktail shaker filled with ice.

2. Shake vigorously until frosted and strain into a chilled cocktail glass. Serve immediately.

SAKETINI

Serves 1

Ingredients

3 measures gin
½ measure sake
ice
lemon peel twist, to decorate

1. Shake the gin and sake vigorously over ice until well frosted.

2. Strain into a chilled cocktail glass and dress with a twist of lemon peel. Serve immediately.

GREEN LADY

Serves 1

Ingredients

2 measures gin
1 measure green Chartreuse
dash lime juice
ice

1. Shake the liquid ingredients vigorously over ice until well frosted.

2. Strain into a chilled cocktail glass and serve immediately.

BACHELOR'S BAIT

Serves 1

Ingredients

2 measures gin

1 tsp grenadine

1 egg white

ice

dash of orange bitters

1. Shake the gin, grenadine and egg white together over ice cubes until well frosted.

2. Add a dash of orange bitters, give the mixture another quick shake and strain into a chilled cocktail glass.
Serve immediately.

CREOLE LADY

Serves 1

Ingredients

2 measures gin

1½ measures Madeira

1 tsp grenadine

cracked ice

cocktail cherries, to decorate

1. Pour the liquid ingredients over ice in a mixing glass.

2. Stir well to mix, then strain into a chilled cocktail glass.

3. Dress with the cocktail cherries and serve immediately.

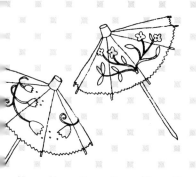

COSMOPOLITAN

Serves 1

Ingredients

4-6 cracked ice cubes
2 measures vodka
1 measure triple sec
1 measure lime juice
1 measure cranberry juice
orange peel strip, to decorate

1. Put the cracked ice cubes into a cocktail shaker.

2. Pour the liquid ingredients over the ice cubes.

3. Shake vigorously until well frosted.

4. Strain into a chilled cocktail glass and decorate with the orange peel. Serve immediately.

WOO-WOO

Serves 1

Ingredients

crushed ice

4 measures cranberry juice

2 measures vodka

2 measures peach schnapps

1. Half fill a chilled cocktail glass with crushed ice.

2. Pour over the cranberry juice.

3. Add the vodka and peach schnapps.

4. Stir well to mix. Serve immediately.

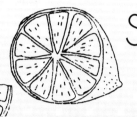

SEX ON THE BEACH

Serves 1

Ingredients

crushed ice

1 measure peach schnapps

1 measure vodka

2 measures fresh orange juice

3 measures cranberry and
peach juice

dash lemon juice

orange peel twist,
to decorate

1. Put 4-6 crushed ice cubes into a cocktail shaker and pour over the peach schnapps, vodka, orange juice and cranberry and peach juice.

2. Shake until well frosted and strain into a glass filled with ice.

3. Squeeze over the lemon juice and decorate with the orange peel. Serve immediately.

SALTY DOG

Serves 1

Ingredients

1 tbsp granulated sugar

1 tbsp coarse salt

1 lime wedge

cracked ice cubes

2 measures vodka

grapefruit juice

1. Mix the sugar and salt in a saucer. Rub the rim of a chilled cocktail glass with the lime wedge and dip into the sugar and salt mixture to coat.

2. Fill the glass with cracked ice cubes and pour over the vodka.

3. Top up with the grapefruit juice and stir. Serve immediately.

FUZZY NAVEL

Serves 1

Ingredients

4-6 cracked ice cubes
2 measures vodka
1 measure peach schnapps
225 ml/8 fl oz orange juice

1. Put the cracked ice cubes into a cocktail shaker.

2. Pour the liquid ingredients over the ice cubes and shake vigorously until well frosted.

3. Strain into a chilled cocktail glass. Serve immediately.

KAMIKAZE

Serves 1

Ingredients

4-6 cracked ice cubes
1 measure vodka
1 measure triple sec
½ measure fresh lime juice
½ measure fresh lemon juice
dry white wine, chilled
cucumber and lime slices,
to decorate

1. Put the cracked ice cubes into a cocktail shaker.

2. Pour over the vodka, triple sec, lime juice and lemon juice and shake until well frosted.

3. Strain into a chilled glass.

4. Top up with wine and decorate with the cucumber and lime slices. Serve immediately.

HARVEY WALLBANGER

Serves 1

Ingredients

cracked ice

3 measures vodka

8 measures orange juice

2 tsp Galliano

cocktail cherry and orange slice, to decorate

1. Half fill a tall glass with cracked ice cubes.

2. Pour over the vodka and orange juice.

3. Float the Galliano on top.

4. Decorate with the cherry and the orange slice. Serve immediately.

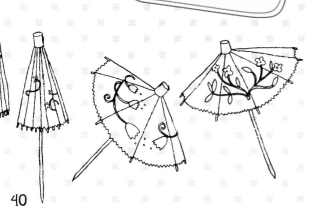

PEARTINI

Serves 1

Ingredients

1 tsp caster sugar
pinch ground cinnamon
1 lemon wedge
4-6 cracked ice cubes
1 measure vodka
1 measure pear brandy

1. Mix the sugar and cinnamon in a saucer.

2. Rub the rim of a cocktail glass with the lemon wedge.

3. Dip into the sugar and cinnamon mixture, to coat.

4. Put the cracked ice cubes into a cocktail shaker and pour in the vodka and pear brandy. Stir well and strain into the glass. Serve immediately.

BLACK BEAUTY

Serves 1

Ingredients

2 measures vodka

1 measure black Sambuca

ice

black olive, to decorate

1. Stir the vodka and Sambuca with ice in a mixing glass until frosted.

2. Strain into a chilled martini glass and dress with the olive. Serve immediately.

SPOTTED BIKINI

Serves 1

Ingredients

1 ripe passion fruit

2 measures vodka

1 measure white rum

1 measure cold milk

juice of ½ lemon

ice

slice of lemon peel,
to decorate

1. Scoop the passion fruit flesh into a jug. Shake the liquid ingredients over ice until well frosted.

2. Strain into a chilled cocktail glass and add the passion fruit at the last minute.

3. Dress with a slice of lemon peel and serve immediately.

CORDLESS SCREWDRIVER

Serves 1

Ingredients

orange wedges

caster sugar

2 measures vodka, chilled

1. Rub the rim of a chilled shot glass with an orange wedge, then dip into a saucer of sugar to frost.

2. Pour the vodka into the glass.

3. Dip an orange wedge into the sugar.

4. Down the vodka in one go and suck the orange.

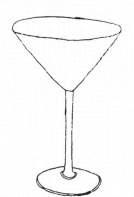

BLUE MONDAY

Serves 1

Ingredients

cracked ice

1 measure vodka

½ measure Cointreau

1 tbsp blue curaçao

1. Put the cracked ice into a mixing glass or jug and pour in the vodka, Cointreau and curaçao.

2. Stir well, strain into a cocktail glass and serve immediately.

BLOODY MARY

Serves 1

Ingredients

4–6 cracked ice cubes

dash hot pepper sauce

dash Worcestershire sauce

2 measures vodka

6 measures tomato juice

juice of ½ lemon

pinch celery salt

pinch cayenne pepper

celery stick and lemon slice,
to decorate

1. Put the cracked ice cubes into a cocktail shaker. Dash the hot pepper sauce and Worcestershire sauce over the ice.

2. Add the vodka, tomato juice and lemon juice and shake vigorously until well frosted.

3. Strain into a tall, chilled glass, add the celery salt and cayenne pepper and decorate with the celery stick and lemon slice. Serve immediately.

Top tip
To make the Canadian favourite Bloody Caesar, simply replace the tomato juice with clamato juice. You can find clamato juice in speciality shops and online.

LONG ISLAND ICED TEA

Serves 1

Ingredients

cracked ice

2 measures vodka

1 measure gin

1 measure white tequila

1 measure white rum

½ measure white crème de menthe

2 measures lemon juice

1 tsp caster sugar

cola

lime wedge, to decorate

1. Put 4–6 cracked ice cubes into a cocktail shaker. Pour all the liquid ingredients except the cola over the ice, add the sugar and shake vigorously until well frosted.

2. Half fill a tall glass with cracked ice and strain over the cocktail.

3. Top up with cola, decorate with the lime wedge and serve immediately.

FLYING GRASSHOPPER

Serves 1

Ingredients

4-6 cracked ice cubes

1 measure vodka

1 measure green crème de
menthe

1 measure crème de cacao

fresh mint, to decorate

1. Put the cracked ice cubes into a mixing glass.

2. Pour over the vodka, crème de menthe and crème de cacao and stir well.

3. Strain into a chilled cocktail glass and decorate with a sprig of fresh mint.
Serve immediately.

AURORA BOREALIS

Serves 1

Ingredients

1 measure chilled grappa or
vodka

1 measure chilled green
Chartreuse

½ measure chilled orange
curaçao

few drops chilled crème
de cassis

1. Pour the grappa slowly over the back of a spoon around one side of a well chilled shot glass.

2. Gently pour the Chartreuse around the other side.

3. Pour the curaçao gently into the middle.

4. Add a few drops of crème de cassis.
Serve immediately.

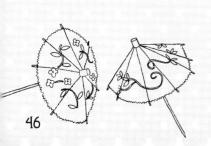

LAST MANGO IN PARIS

Serves 1

Ingredients

2 measures vodka

1 measure framboise

1 measure lime juice

½ mango, peeled, stoned, and chopped

2 halved strawberries

lime slice, to decorate

1. Mix the ingredients in a blender until slushy.

2. Pour into a chilled glass and dress with a slice of lime. Serve immediately.

THUNDERBIRD

Serves 1

Ingredients

2 measures iced vodka

dash Parfait Amour

dash cassis

small piece of orange zest

one rose or violet petal

1. Pour the vodka into a frosted martini glass.

2. Add the other ingredients slowly and stir only once. Serve immediately.

MIMI

Serves 1

Ingredients

2 measures vodka
½ measure coconut cream
2 measures pineapple juice
4-6 crushed ice cubes
fresh pineapple slice,
to decorate

1. Put the vodka, coconut cream, pineapple juice and crushed ice in a blender.

2. Blend for a few seconds until frothy.

3. Pour into a chilled cocktail glass.

4. Decorate with a slice of pineapple. Serve immediately.

3

4

SUNNY BAY

Serves 1

Ingredients

1½ measures vodka

½ measure melon liqueur

2 measures pineapple juice

cracked ice

maraschino cherry,
to decorate

1. Pour the ingredients into a shaker filled with ice.

2. Shake well.

3. Strain into a chilled cocktail glass, and dress with the cherry on a cocktail stick. Serve immediately.

SEABREEZE

Serves 1

Ingredients

4–6 cracked ice cubes
1½ measures vodka
½ measure cranberry juice
pink grapefruit juice

1. Put the cracked ice cubes into a cocktail shaker.

2. Pour over the vodka and cranberry juice and shake until frosted.

3. Strain into a chilled tumbler and top up with pink grapefruit juice. Serve immediately.

CRANBERRY COLLINS

Serves 1

Ingredients

cracked ice cubes
2 measures vodka
¾ measure elderflower cordial
3 measures cranberry juice
soda water
lime slice and lime peel twist,
to decorate

1. Put 4–6 cracked ice cubes into a cocktail shaker.

2. Pour over the vodka, elderflower cordial and cranberry juice and shake until well frosted.

3. Strain into a Collins glass filled with cracked ice.

4. Top up with soda water and decorate with the lime slice and peel. Serve immediately.

MOSCOW MULE

Serves 1

Ingredients

cracked ice
2 measures vodka
1 measure lime juice
ginger beer
lime wedge, to decorate

1. Put 4–6 cracked ice cubes into a cocktail shaker.

2. Pour the vodka and lime juice over the ice cubes and shake vigorously until well frosted.

3. Half fill a chilled glass with cracked ice and strain over the cocktail.

4. Top up with ginger beer and decorate with the lime wedge. Serve immediately.

SCREWDRIVER

Serves 1

Ingredients

cracked ice
2 measures vodka
orange juice
orange slice, to decorate

1. Fill a tall, chilled glass with cracked ice. Pour the vodka over the ice.

2. Top up with orange juice and stir well to mix.

3. Decorate with the orange slice. Serve immediately.

METROPOLITAN

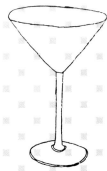

Serves 1

Ingredients

1 lemon wedge

1 tbsp caster sugar

4-6 cracked ice cubes

½ measure vodka

½ measure framboise liqueur

½ measure cranberry juice

½ measure orange juice

1. Rub the rim of a cocktail glass with the lemon wedge.

2. Dip into the sugar, to coat.

3. Put the cracked ice cubes into a cocktail shaker and pour over the liquid ingredients.

4. Cover and shake vigorously until well frosted. Strain into the glass and serve immediately.

2

1

4

VODKA ESPRESSO

Serves 1

Ingredients

4-6 cracked ice cubes

2 measures espresso or other strong black coffee, cooled

1 measure vodka

2 tsp caster sugar

1 measure Amarula

1. Put the cracked ice into a cocktail shaker.

2. Pour in the coffee and vodka, add the sugar and shake vigorously until well frosted.

3. Strain into a chilled cocktail glass.

4. Float the Amarula on top. Serve immediately.

3

2

4

PIÑA COLADA

Serves 1

Ingredients

4-6 crushed ice cubes

2 measures white rum

1 measure dark rum

3 measures pineapple juice

2 measures coconut cream

cocktail cherry and pineapple wedge, to decorate

1. Put the crushed ice cubes in a blender. Pour over the white rum, dark rum and pineapple juice.

2. Add the coconut cream to the blender and blend until smooth.

3. Pour, without straining, into a chilled glass.

4. Decorate with the cocktail cherry and the pineapple wedge.

5. Serve immediately.

CLUB MOJITO

Serves 1

Ingredients

1 tsp sugar syrup

6 fresh mint leaves,
plus extra to decorate

juice of ½ lime

4–6 cracked ice cubes

2 measures Jamaican rum

soda water

dash Angostura bitters

1. Put the sugar syrup, mint leaves and lime juice into a lowball glass.

2. Muddle the mint leaves, then add the cracked ice cubes and the rum.

3. Top up with soda water.

4. Finish with the Angostura bitters and decorate with the remaining mint leaves.

5. Serve immediately.

2

3

5

BAJAN SUN

Serves 1

Ingredients

4-6 crushed ice cubes

1 measure white rum

1 measure mandarin brandy

1 measure fresh orange juice

1 measure pineapple juice

splash of grenadine

fresh pineapple slice and a cocktail cherry, to decorate

1. Put the crushed ice into a cocktail shaker.

2. Pour over the rum, brandy, orange juice and pineapple juice.

3. Add the grenadine and shake vigorously.

4. Strain into a tall, chilled glass and decorate with the pineapple slice and cocktail cherry. Serve immediately.

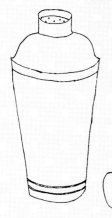

PLANTATION PUNCH

Serves 1

Ingredients

4-6 cracked ice cubes

2 measures dark rum

1 measure Southern Comfort

1 measure lemon juice

1 tsp brown sugar

sparkling water

1 tsp ruby port

1. Put the cracked ice cubes into a cocktail shaker. Add the rum, Southern Comfort, lemon juice and brown sugar.

2. Shake vigorously until well frosted. Strain into a tall, chilled glass. Top up with sparkling water.

3. Float the port on top by pouring it gently over the back of a teaspoon. Serve immediately.

OCEAN BREEZE

Serves 1

Ingredients

4-6 crushed ice cubes
1 measure white rum
1 measure amaretto
½ measure blue curaçao
½ measure pineapple juice
soda water

1. Put the crushed ice into a cocktail shaker.

2. Pour over the white rum, amaretto, blue curaçao and pineapple juice and shake well.

3. Strain into a tall, chilled glass and top up with soda water. Serve immediately.

BLUE HAWAIIAN

Serves 1

Ingredients

4-6 crushed ice cubes
2 measures Bacardi rum
½ measure blue curaçao
1 measure pineapple juice
½ measure coconut cream
pineapple wedge, to decorate

1. Put the crushed ice in a cocktail shaker.

2. Pour over the liquid ingredients. Shake vigorously until well frosted and strain into a chilled wine glass.

3. Decorate with the pineapple wedge. Serve immediately.

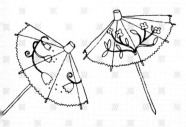

BANANA COLADA

Serves 1

Ingredients

4-6 ice cubes, crushed

2 measures white rum

4 measures pineapple juice

1 measure Malibu

1 banana, peeled and sliced

pineapple wedges

1. Whizz the crushed ice in a blender with the white rum, pineapple juice, Malibu and sliced banana.

2. Blend until smooth, then pour, without straining, into a chilled highball glass and serve immediately with pineapple wedges and a straw.

Top tip
Use frozen bananas for a super-cold treat on a hot day.

STRAWBERRY COLADA

Serves 1

Ingredients

4-6 crushed ice cubes

3 measures golden rum

4 measures pineapple juice

1 measure coconut cream

6 strawberries

pineapple wedge, and halved strawberry, to decorate

1. Put the crushed ice in a blender. Add the rum, pineapple juice and coconut cream.

2. Hull the strawberries and add to the blender. Blend until smooth and pour, without straining, into a tall, chilled tumbler.

3. Decorate with the pineapple wedge and strawberry and serve immediately.

CUBA LIBRE

Serves 1

Ingredients

cracked ice

2 measures white rum

cola

lime wedge, to decorate

1. Half fill a highball glass with cracked ice.

2. Pour over the rum and top up with cola.

3. Stir gently to mix and decorate with the lime wedge.
Serve immediately.

CUBAN SPECIAL

Serves 1

Ingredients

4-6 cracked ice cubes

2 measures white rum

1 measure lime juice

1 tbsp pineapple juice

1 tsp triple sec

pineapple wedges, to decorate

1. Put the cracked ice cubes into a cocktail shaker.

2. Pour over the rum, lime juice, pineapple juice and triple sec. Shake vigorously until well frosted. Strain into a chilled cocktail glass.

3. Decorate with the pineapple wedges and serve immediately.

RUM NOGGIN

Serves 8

Ingredients

6 eggs

4–5 tsp icing sugar

freshly grated nutmeg,
plus extra for sprinkling

475 ml/16 fl oz dark rum

2 litres/2 pints milk, warmed

1. Blend the eggs in a punch bowl with the sugar and a little nutmeg.

2. Whisk in the rum and gradually stir in the milk.

3. Warm through gently, if you wish, and serve immediately in small heatproof glasses or mugs, sprinkled with nutmeg.

RUM COBBLER

Serves 1

Ingredients

1 tsp icing sugar

2 measures sparkling water

cracked ice

2 measures white rum

lime slice and orange slice,
to decorate

1. Put the sugar into a chilled goblet. Add the sparkling water and stir until the sugar has dissolved.

2. Fill the glass with ice and pour in the rum. Stir well and dress with a lime slice and an orange slice. Serve immediately.

FROZEN PEACH DAIQUIRI

Serves 1

Ingredients

4–6 crushed ice cubes
½ peach, stoned and chopped
2 measures white rum
1 measure lime juice
1 tsp sugar syrup
peach slice, to decorate

1. Put the crushed ice and the peach into a blender.

2. Add the rum, lime juice and sugar syrup and blend until slushy.

3. Pour into a chilled cocktail glass.

4. Decorate with the peach slice.

5. Serve immediately.

RUM COOLER

Serves 1

Ingredients

cracked ice

1½ measures white rum

1½ measures pineapple juice

1 banana, peeled and sliced

juice of 1 lime

lime peel twist, to decorate

1. Put 2–4 cracked ice cubes, the rum, pineapple juice and banana into a blender.

2. Add the lime juice and blend for about 1 minute or until smooth.

3. Fill a chilled glass with cracked ice and pour over the cocktail.

4. Decorate with the lime peel.

5. Serve immediately.

2

1

5

WHISKEY SOUR

Serves 1

Ingredients

4–6 cracked ice cubes

2 measures American blended whiskey

1 measure lime juice

1 tsp icing sugar or sugar syrup

lime slice and cocktail cherry, to decorate

1. Put the cracked ice cubes into a cocktail shaker and pour over the whiskey.

2. Add the lime juice and sugar and shake well.

3. Strain into a cocktail glass and decorate with the slice of lime and a cherry. Serve immediately.

WHISKEY RICKEY

Serves 1

Ingredients

4–6 crushed ice cubes

2 measures American blended whiskey

1 measure lime juice

soda water

lime slice, to decorate

1. Put the crushed ice into a chilled highball glass.

2. Pour over the whiskey and lime juice and top up with soda water.

3. Stir gently to mix, decorate with the lime slice and serve immediately.

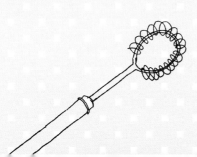

HIGHLAND FLING

Serves 1

Ingredients

4-6 cracked ice cubes

dash of Angostura bitters

2 measures Scotch whisky

1 measure sweet vermouth

cocktail olive, to decorate

1. Put the cracked ice into a mixing glass.

2. Pour over the Angostura bitters. Pour in the whisky and vermouth and stir well to mix.

3. Strain into a chilled glass and decorate with the olive. Serve immediately.

WHISKEY SLING

Serves 1

Ingredients

1 tsp icing sugar

1 measure lemon juice

1 tsp water

2 measures American blended whiskey

cracked ice

orange wedge, to decorate

1. Put the sugar into a mixing glass.

2. Add the lemon juice and water and stir until the sugar has dissolved.

3. Pour in the whiskey and stir to mix.

4. Half fill a small chilled tumbler with cracked ice and strain the cocktail over it.

5. Decorate with the orange wedge and serve immediately.

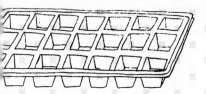

MIAMI BEACH

Serves 1

Ingredients

4-6 cracked ice cubes

2 measures Scotch whisky

1½ measures dry vermouth

2 measures pink grapefruit juice

orange peel strip, to decorate

1. Put the cracked ice cubes into a cocktail shaker.

2. Pour over the whisky, vermouth and grapefruit juice.

3. Shake vigorously until well frosted. Strain into a chilled cocktail glass.

4. Decorate with the orange peel strip and serve immediately.

BOSTON SOUR

Serves 1

Ingredients

4-6 cracked ice cubes

1 measure lemon juice or lime juice

2 measures American blended whiskey

1 tsp sugar syrup

1 egg white

lemon slice and cocktail cherry, to decorate

1. Put the cracked ice cubes into a cocktail shaker.

2. Pour over the lemon juice, whiskey and sugar syrup.

3. Add the egg white.

4. Shake until chilled. Strain into a cocktail glass and decorate with the lemon slice and a cocktail cherry. Serve immediately.

KLONDIKE COOLER

Serves 1

Ingredients

½ tsp icing sugar

1 measure ginger ale

cracked ice

2 measures blended whiskey

sparkling water

lemon peel twist, to decorate

1. Put the sugar into a chilled tumbler and add the ginger ale. Stir until the sugar has dissolved.

2. Fill the glass with cracked ice. Pour over the whiskey.

3. Top up with sparkling water. Stir gently and decorate with the lemon peel. Serve immediately.

SHAMROCK

Serves 1

Ingredients

4-6 cracked ice cubes

1 measure Irish whiskey

1 measure dry vermouth

3 dashes of green Chartreuse

3 dashes of crème de menthe

1. Put the cracked ice into a mixing glass.

2. Pour over the whiskey, vermouth and Chartreuse. Stir until well frosted.

3. Strain into a chilled cocktail glass, pour over the crème de menthe and stir. Serve immediately.

MANHATTAN

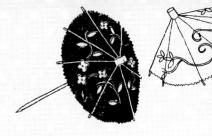

Serves 1

Ingredients

4–6 cracked ice cubes

dash Angostura bitters

3 measures rye whiskey

1 measure sweet vermouth

cocktail cherry, to decorate

1. Put the cracked ice cubes into a cocktail shaker.

2. Pour the liquid ingredients over the ice cubes and shake vigorously until well frosted.

3. Strain into a chilled cocktail glass and decorate with the cherry. Serve immediately.

OLD-FASHIONED

Serves 1

Ingredients

1 sugar cube

dash of Angostura bitters

1 tsp water

2 measures bourbon or rye whiskey

4–6 cracked ice cubes

lemon peel twist, to decorate

1. Place the sugar cube in a small, chilled lowball glass.

2. Add the Angostura bitters and water. Stir until the sugar has dissolved.

3. Pour in the bourbon and stir.

4. Add the cracked ice cubes and decorate with the lemon peel. Serve immediately.

WHISKEY SANGAREE

Serves 1

Ingredients

4–6 ice cubes

2 measures bourbon

1 tsp sugar syrup

soda water

1 tbsp ruby port

freshly grated nutmeg,
to decorate

1. Put the ice in a chilled tumbler.

2. Pour over the bourbon and sugar syrup. Top up with soda water.

3. Stir gently to mix, then float the port on top. Sprinkle over some of the grated nutmeg. Serve immediately.

Top tip
Instead of bourbon whiskey, try a blended whiskey, or indeed any whiskey of your choice in this cocktail classic.

PINK HEATHER

Serves 1

Ingredients

1 measure Scotch whisky

1 measure strawberry liqueur

chilled sparkling wine

fresh strawberry, to decorate

1. Pour the whisky and the strawberry liqueur into a chilled champagne flute.

2. Top up with chilled sparkling wine and dress with a strawberry. Serve immediately.

FLYING SCOTSMAN

Serves 1

Ingredients

crushed ice
dash Angostura bitters
2 measures Scotch whisky
1 measure sweet vermouth
¼ tsp sugar syrup

1. Put some crushed ice into a blender.

2. Dash Angostura bitters over the ice, and add the whisky, vermouth and sugar syrup.

3. Blend until slushy and pour into a small chilled tumbler. Serve immediately.

BEADLESTONE

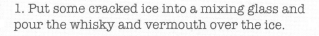

Serves 1

Ingredients

cracked ice
2 measures Scotch whisky
1½ measures dry vermouth

1. Put some cracked ice into a mixing glass and pour the whisky and vermouth over the ice.

2. Stir well to mix and strain into a chilled cocktail glass. Serve immediately.

THISTLE

Serves 1

Ingredients

cracked ice

dash Angostura bitters

2 measures Scotch whisky

1½ measures sweet vermouth

1. Put some cracked ice into a mixing glass.

2. Dash Angostura bitters over the ice and pour in the whisky and vermouth.

3. Stir well to mix and strain into a chilled cocktail glass. Serve immediately.

COLLEEN

Serves 1

Ingredients

2 measures Irish whiskey

1 measure Irish Mist

1 measure triple sec

1 tsp lemon juice

ice

1. Shake the liquid ingredients vigorously over ice until well frosted.

2. Strain into a chilled cocktail glass. Serve immediately.

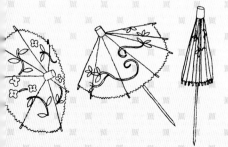

THE REVIVER

Serves 1

Ingredients

⅓ measure brandy
⅓ measure Fernet Branca
⅓ measure crème de menthe
ice

1. Shake the liquids well over ice until frosted.

2. Strain into a cocktail glass and drink as quickly as possible.

Fact
This cocktail, as its name suggests, is supposed to revive after a night of heavy drinking!

MIDNIGHT COWBOY

Serves 1

Ingredients

1 measure brandy

½ measure coffee liqueur

½ measure cream, chilled

crushed ice

cola

1. Slowly blend together the brandy, coffee liqueur, cream and ice in a blender until frothy.

2. Pour into a chilled long glass. Top up with cola and serve immediately.

CUBAN

Serves 1

Ingredients

2 measures brandy

1 measure apricot brandy

1 measure lime juice

1 tsp white rum

ice

1. Pour the liquid ingredients over ice and shake vigorously until well frosted.

2. Strain into a chilled cocktail glass and serve immediately.

BRANDY SOUR

Serves 1

Ingredients

1 measure lemon or lime juice

2½ measures brandy

1 tsp icing sugar or sugar syrup

ice

lime slice and maraschino cherry, to decorate

1. Shake the lemon juice, brandy and sugar well over ice and strain into a cocktail glass.

2. Dress with a lime slice and a cherry and serve immediately.

SIDECAR

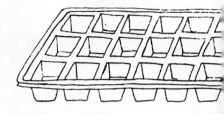

Serves 1

Ingredients

4–6 cracked ice cubes

2 measures brandy

1 measure triple sec

1 measure lemon juice

orange peel twist,
to decorate

1. Put the cracked ice cubes into a cocktail shaker. Pour the liquid ingredients over the ice cubes.

2. Shake vigorously until well frosted.

3. Strain into a chilled cocktail glass and decorate with the orange peel. Serve immediately.

BRANDY JULEP

Serves 1

Ingredients

cracked ice

2 measures brandy

1 tsp sugar syrup

4 fresh mint leaves

fresh mint sprig and
lemon slice, to decorate

1. Fill a chilled lowball glass with cracked ice.

2. Add the brandy, sugar syrup and mint leaves, and stir well to mix.

3. Dress the cocktail with a sprig of fresh mint and a slice of lemon. Serve immediately.

PINK WHISKERS

Serves 1

Ingredients

2 measures apricot brandy

1 measure dry vermouth

2 measures orange juice

dash grenadine

ice

1. Shake the liquid ingredients vigorously over ice until well frosted.

2. Strain the mixture into a chilled cocktail glass and serve immediately.

Top tip
Float 30 ml/2 tbsp of port on top for an extra depth and flavour.

FIRST NIGHT

Serves 1

Ingredients

2 measures brandy

1 measure Van der Hum

1 measure Tia Maria

1 tsp cream

ice

grated chocolate, to decorate

1. Shake the liquid ingredients together over ice.

2. Strain into a chilled cocktail glass and dress with a little grated chocolate. Serve immediately.

HEAVENLY

Serves 1

Ingredients

cracked ice

1½ measures brandy

½ measure cherry brandy

½ measure plum brandy

maraschino cherries,
to decorate

1. Put the ice in a mixing glass.

2. Pour the liquid ingredients over the ice and stir well to mix.

3. Strain into a chilled cocktail glass and dress with cherries. Serve immediately.

CHERRY KITSCH

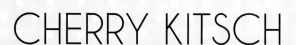

Serves 1

Ingredients

1 measure cherry brandy

2 measures pineapple juice

½ measure kirsch

1 egg white

crushed ice

frozen maraschino cherry,
to decorate

1. Shake the cherry brandy, pineapple juice, kirsch and egg white well over ice until frosted.

2. Pour into a chilled tall thin glass and top with a frozen maraschino cherry. Serve immediately.

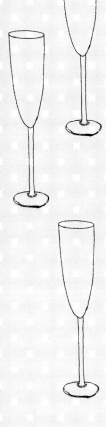

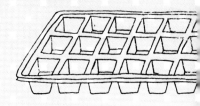

GODDAUGHTER

Serves 1

Ingredients

crushed ice

2 measures apple brandy

1 measure amaretto

1 tsp apple sauce

ground cinnamon, to decorate

1. Put some crushed ice into a blender and add the apple brandy, amaretto and apple sauce.

2. Blend until smooth, then pour the mixture, without straining, into a chilled glass.

3. Sprinkle with ground cinnamon and serve immediately.

BEAGLE

Serves 1

Ingredients

cracked ice

dash kümmel

dash lemon juice

2 measures brandy

1 measure cranberry juice

1. Put cracked ice into a mixing glass.

2. Dash kümmel and lemon juice over the ice and pour in the brandy and cranberry juice.

3. Stir well to mix, strain into a chilled cocktail glass and serve immediately.

BRANDY ALEXANDER

Serves 1

Ingredients

4-6 cracked ice cubes

1 measure brandy

1 measure dark crème de cacao

1 measure double cream

freshly grated nutmeg, to decorate

1. Put the cracked ice cubes into a cocktail shaker.

2. Pour over the brandy, crème de cacao and cream and shake vigorously until well frosted.

3. Strain into a chilled cocktail glass. Sprinkle over the grated nutmeg and serve immediately.

Top tip
This is the perfect after dinner cocktail to serve with a creamy, chocolaty dessert.

HOT BRANDY CHOCOLATE

Serves 4

Ingredients

1 litre/1¾ pints milk

115 g/4 oz plain chocolate, broken into pieces

2 tbsp sugar

4 measures brandy

6 tbsp whipped cream

freshly grated nutmeg or cocoa powder, for sprinkling

1. Heat the milk in a small pan to just below boiling point.

2. Add the chocolate and sugar and stir over a low heat until the chocolate has melted.

3. Pour into four warmed heatproof glasses, then pour 1 measure of the brandy over the back of a spoon on top of each.

4. Add the whipped cream and sprinkle over the grated nutmeg. Serve immediately.

KIR ROYALE

Serves 1

Ingredients

few drops crème de cassis,
or to taste

½ measure brandy

champagne, chilled

fresh mint spring, to decorate

1. Put the cassis into the bottom of a champagne flute.

2. Add the brandy. Top up with champagne.

3. Decorate with the mint sprig and serve immediately.

DISCO DANCER

Serves 1

Ingredients

1 measure crème de banane

1 measure rum

few drops Angostura bitters

ice

sparkling white wine

1. Shake the first three ingredients well over ice.

2. Pour into a chilled glass and top up with sparkling wine to taste. Serve immediately.

DIAMOND FIZZ

Serves 1

Ingredients

2 measures gin

½ measure lemon juice

1 tsp sugar syrup

ice

chilled champagne

1. Shake the gin, lemon juice and sugar syrup over ice until well frosted.

2. Strain into a chilled flute. Top up with chilled champagne and serve immediately.

CHAMPAGNE SIDECAR

Serves 1

Ingredients

1½ measures bourbon

1 measure Cointreau

¼ measure lemon juice

ice

chilled champagne

1. Shake the bourbon, Cointreau and lemon juice over ice and strain into a chilled flute.

2. Top up with chilled champagne and serve immediately.

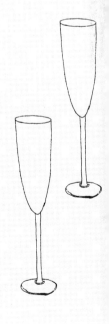

CHAMPAGNE COCKTAIL

Serves 1

Ingredients

1 sugar cube
2 dashes Angostura bitters
1 measure brandy
champagne, chilled

1. Place the sugar cube in the bottom of a chilled champagne flute.

2. Add the Angostura bitters and the brandy.

3. Top up with champagne and serve immediately.

CHAMPAGNE PICK-ME-UP

Serves 1

Ingredients

4–6 cracked ice cubes

2 measures brandy

1 measure orange juice

1 measure lemon juice

dash grenadine

champagne, chilled

1. Put the cracked ice cubes into a cocktail shaker.

2. Pour over the brandy, orange juice, lemon juice and grenadine and shake vigorously until well frosted.

3. Strain into a chilled wine glass, top up with champagne and serve immediately.

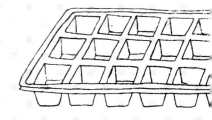

BUCK'S FIZZ

Serves 1

Ingredients

2 measures chilled fresh
orange juice

2 measures champagne,
chilled

1. Half fill a chilled flute with orange juice, then gently pour in the chilled champagne. Serve immediately.

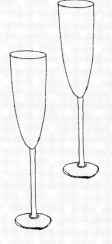

DUKE

Serves 1

Ingredients

1 measure triple sec

½ measure lemon juice

½ measure orange juice

1 egg white

dash maraschino liqueur

cracked ice cubes

champagne or sparkling wine,
chilled

1. Shake the triple sec, lemon juice, orange juice, egg white and maraschino liqueur vigorously over cracked ice until well frosted.

2. Strain into a chilled wine glass and top up with chilled champagne.
Serve immediately.

KISMET

Serves 1

Ingredients

1 measure gin

1 measure apricot brandy

½ tsp stem ginger syrup

champagne, chilled

fresh mango slices, to decorate

1. Pour the gin and brandy into a chilled flute.

2. Trickle the ginger syrup slowly down the glass and then top up with champagne. Dress with a slice of mango and serve immediately.

LONDON FRENCH 75

Serves 1

Ingredients

2 measures London gin

1 measure lemon juice

cracked ice cubes

champagne, chilled

1. Shake the gin and lemon juice vigorously over cracked ice until well frosted.

2. Strain into a chilled glass and top up with champagne. Serve immediately.

BELLINI

Serves 1

Ingredients

1 lemon wedge

caster sugar

1 measure peach juice

3 measures champagne, chilled

1. Rub the rim of a chilled champagne flute with the lemon wedge.

2. Put the sugar in a saucer, then dip the rim of the flute in it.

3. Pour the peach juice into the flute.

4. Top up with the champagne.

5. Serve immediately.

3

1

5

MIMOSA

Serves 1

Ingredients

cracked ice
1 passion fruit
½ measure orange curaçao
champagne, chilled
star fruit slice, to decorate

1. Put the cracked ice cubes into a cocktail shaker.

2. Scoop out the passion fruit flesh into the shaker.

3. Add the curaçao and shake until frosted.

4. Strain into a chilled champagne flute, top up with champagne and decorate with the star fruit slice.

5. Serve immediately.

3

2

5

SAN REMO

Serves 1

Ingredients

½ measure grapefruit juice

¼ measure triple sec

¼ measure mandarin liqueur

ice

champagne, chilled

frozen citrus fruit slices,
to decorate

1. Mix the first three ingredients with ice in a tall glass.

2. Top up with champagne and dress with slices of frozen fruit. Serve immediately.

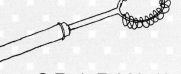

SPARKLING GOLD

Serves 1

Ingredients

1 measure golden rum

½ measure Cointreau

chilled champagne

1. Pour the rum and liqueur into a chilled flute and top up with champagne. Serve immediately.

THE BENTLEY

Serves 1

Ingredients

½ measure cognac or brandy

½ measure peach liqueur, peach brandy or schnapps

juice of 1 passion fruit, sieved

1 ice cube

champagne, chilled

1. Mix the first three ingredients gently together in a chilled glass.

2. Add one ice cube and slowly pour in champagne to taste. Serve immediately.

RASPBERRY MIST

Serves 24

Ingredients

6 measures Irish Mist honey liqueur

450 g/1 lb raspberries

55 g/2 oz crushed ice

4 bottles sparkling dry white wine, well chilled

24 raspberries, to decorate

1. Blend the liqueur and raspberries in a blender with the crushed ice.

2. When lightly frozen, strain between chilled champagne bowls and top up with wine.

3. Top each glass with a raspberry and serve immediately.

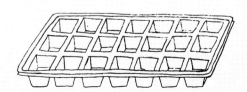

WILD SILK

Serves 2

Ingredients

a few raspberries

½ measure cream

1 measure framboise or
raspberry syrup

crushed ice

champagne, chilled

1. Set aside 2 nice raspberries. Blend the remainder with the cream, framboise and a little ice in a blender until frosted and slushy.

2. Pour into a chilled glass and top up with champagne.

3. Float a raspberry on top and serve immediately.

BLACK VELVET

Serves 1

Ingredients

stout, chilled

sparkling white wine, chilled

1. Half fill a tumbler with stout, then very slowly pour in an equal quantity of wine over the back of a spoon that is just touching the top of the stout and the edge of the glass. Serve immediately.

Top tip
Pouring the wine over the back of a spoon as described here should stop the drinks from mixing together and keep them in separate layers.

ROYAL JULEP

Serves 1

Ingredients

1 sugar lump

3 sprigs fresh mint,
plus extra to decorate

1 measure Jack Daniels
whiskey

champagne, chilled

1. In a small glass, crush the sugar and mint together with a little of the whiskey.

2. When the sugar has dissolved, strain it into a chilled flute with the rest of the whiskey, and top up with champagne.

3. Dress with a mint sprig and serve immediately.

CARIBBEAN CHAMPAGNE

Serves 1

Ingredients

½ measure white rum

½ measure crème de banane

champagne, chilled

banana slices, to decorate

1. Pour the rum and crème de banane into a chilled flute and top up with champagne.

2. Stir gently to mix and dress with slices of banana. Serve immediately.

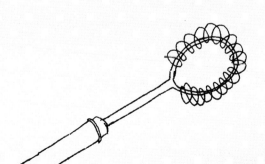

JADE

Serves 1

Ingredients

¼ measure Midori

¼ measure blue curaçao

¼ measure lime juice

dash Angostura bitters

cracked ice

champagne, chilled

lime slice, to decorate

1. Shake the Midori, curaçao, lime juice and Angostura bitters vigorously over ice until well frosted.

2. Strain into a chilled flute. Top up with chilled champagne and dress with a slice of lime. Serve immediately.

UNDER THE BOARDWALK

Serves 1

Ingredients

crushed ice

2 measures lemon juice

½ tsp sugar syrup

½ peach, peeled, stoned and chopped

sparkling water

raspberries, to decorate

1. Blend crushed ice in a blender with the lemon juice, sugar syrup, and chopped peach until slushy.

2. Pour into a chilled tumbler, top up with sparkling water and stir gently.

3. Dress with raspberries and serve immediately.

MONTE CARLO

Serves 1

Ingredients

4–6 ice cubes
½ measure gin
¼ measure lemon juice
champagne or sparkling white wine, chilled
¼ measure crème de menthe
fresh mint sprig, to decorate

1. Put the ice into a mixing glass, pour over the gin and lemon juice.

2. Stir until well chilled.

3. Strain into a chilled champagne flute and top up with champagne.

4. Drizzle the crème de menthe over the top and decorate with the mint sprig.

5. Serve immediately.

FLIRTINI

Serves 1

Ingredients

¼ slice fresh pineapple,
chopped

½ measure chilled Cointreau

½ measure chilled vodka

1 measure chilled pineapple
juice

champagne, chilled

1. Put the pineapple into a mixing glass or jug.

2. Crush the pineapple and add the Cointreau, vodka
and pineapple juice. Stir well.

3. Strain into a glass and top up with champagne.

4. Serve immediately.

2

3

4

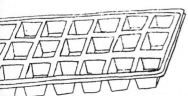

PEACEMAKER

Serves 4

Ingredients

25 strawberries, hulled

½ small fresh pineapple, peeled and crushed

1–2 tbsp icing sugar

1 measure maraschino

225 ml/8 fl oz sparkling water

1 bottle dry champagne

fresh mint leaves and sliced strawberries, to decorate

1. Put the fruit and sugar into a large punch bowl.

2. Add a little water and crush together.

3. Add the maraschino and sparkling water and mix well.

4. Top up with the champagne and decorate with the mint leaves and strawberry slices. Serve immediately.

SOUTHERN CHAMPAGNE

Serves 1

Ingredients

1 measure Southern Comfort

dash Angostura aromatic bitters

champagne, chilled

twist of orange rind, to decorate

1. Pour the liqueur and bitters into a chilled champagne flute, and stir to mix.

2. Fill the glass with champagne. Drop the rind into the glass, to decorate and serve immediately.

AMARETTINE

Serves 1

Ingredients

⅓ measure amaretto

⅓ measure dry vermouth

sparkling white wine

1. Mix the amaretto and vermouth in a chilled tall cocktail glass. Top up with wine to taste and serve immediately.

SABRINA

Serves 1

Ingredients

½ measure gin

⅛ measure apricot brandy

½ measure fresh orange juice

1 tsp grenadine

¼ measure Cinzano

ice

sweet sparkling wine

orange and lemon slices,
to decorate

1. Shake the first five ingredients together over ice.

2. Pour into a tall glass and top up with sparkling wine.

3. Dress with slices of orange and lemon and serve immediately.

PINK SHERBET ROYALE

Serves 2

Ingredients

1½ cups sparkling white wine, really cold

2 measures crème de cassis

1 measure brandy

crushed ice

blackberries, to decorate

1. Blend half the wine in a blender with the cassis, brandy and ice until really cold and frosted.

2. Slowly whisk in a little more wine and pour into tall thin glasses.

3. Dress with the blackberries and serve immediately.

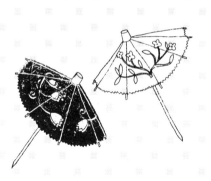

KIR LETHALE

Serves 1

Ingredients

1 raisin soaked in vodka
½ measure crème de cassis
1 tsp vodka
sparkling wine

1. Put the raisin in the bottom of a chilled champagne flute.

2. Pour in the crème de cassis and vodka.

3. Fill the glass with sparkling wine and serve immediately.

BROKEN NEGRONI

Serves 1

Ingredients

1 measure sweet vermouth

1 measure Campari bitters

ice

sparkling wine

half a thin slice of orange,
to decorate

1. Add the vermouth and bitters to a mixing glass filled with ice, and stir.

2. Strain into a chilled champagne flute.

3. Top with sparkling wine, and dress the glass with the orange slice. Serve immediately.

SEELBACH

Serves 1

Ingredients

½ measure bourbon

¼ measure triple sec

2 dashes Angostura aromatic bitters

2 dashes Peychaud's aromatic bitters

sparkling wine

orange twist, to decorate

1. Pour the bourbon and triple sec into a chilled champagne flute.

2. Add the bitters.

3. Top with sparkling wine.

4. Dress the glass with the orange twist and serve immediately.

DEATH IN THE AFTERNOON

Serves 1

Ingredients

1 measure pastis

sparkling wine

twist of lemon, to decorate

1. Pour the pastis into a chilled champagne flute.

2. Top with sparkling wine.

3. Dress the glass with the lemon twist and serve immediately.

THE QUEENS COUSIN

Serves 1

Ingredients

1 measure vodka

½ measure orange-flavoured liqueur

½ measure fresh lime juice

1 tsp triple sec

dash Angostura aromatic bitters

cracked ice

sparkling wine

1. Pour the vodka, orange-flavoured liqueur, fresh lime juice, triple sec and bitters into a shaker filled with ice.

2. Shake well and strain into a chilled wine glass

3. Fill the glass with sparkling wine and serve immediately.

MIDNIGHT'S KISS

Serves 1

Ingredients

sugar

wedge of lemon

½ measure vodka

2 tsp blue curaçao

cracked ice

sparkling wine

1. Spread the sugar on a plate. Run a wedge of lemon around the rim of a chilled champagne flute to moisten it, and then dip the glass in the sugar.

2. Add the vodka and curaçao to a shaker filled with ice.

3. Shake well, strain into the glass and top with sparkling wine. Serve immediately.

Top tip
You can use any sugar for rimming the glass — or buy gold sugar from a specialist supplier to increase the glamour factor of this cocktail.

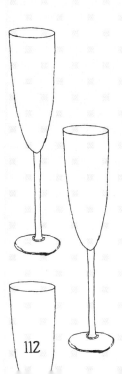

PRETTY IN PINK

Serves 1

Ingredients

1 measure lemonade
1 measure cranberry juice
ice
sparkling wine
sprig of mint, to decorate

1. Pour the lemonade and juice into a lowball glass filled with ice.

2. Stir gently.

3. Fill the glass to the top with sparkling wine.

4. Decorate with the mint sprig and serve immediately.

SAN JOAQUIN PUNCH

Serves 4

Ingredients

1 tbsp raisins or chopped prunes

6 tsp brandy

300 ml/10 fl oz sparkling white wine or champagne, chilled

300 ml/10 fl oz white cranberry and grape juice

ice cubes

1. Mix the dried fruit and brandy in a small bowl and leave to soak for 1–2 hours.

2. In a jug, mix the sparkling wine, juice and brandy-soaked fruit.

3. Pour into ice-filled glasses and serve immediately.

ROYAL SILVER

Serves 1

Ingredients

grenadine

sugar

½ measure pear liqueur

½ measure triple sec

2 measures grapefruit juice

cracked ice

sparkling wine

1. Dip the rim of a wine glass first into some grenadine and then into some sugar.

2. Pour the pear liqueur, triple sec and juice into a shaker filled with ice.

3. Shake well and strain carefully into a chilled glass.

4. Top with sparkling wine and serve immediately.

MARILYN MONROE

Serves 1

Ingredients

1 measure apple brandy

1 tsp grenadine

sparkling wine

2 cocktail cherries, to decorate

1. Add the brandy and grenadine to a chilled champagne saucer and stir.

2. Top with sparkling wine.

3. Hang the cherries over the edge of the glass to decorate and serve immediately.

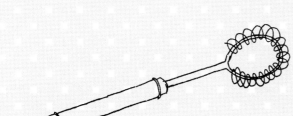

NIGHT & DAY

Serves 1

Ingredients

3 measures sparkling wine

3 tsp brandy

2 tsp orange-flavoured liqueur

1 tsp Campari bitters

1. Pour the sparkling wine into a chilled champagne flute.

2. Slowly add the brandy and the orange-flavoured liqueur, then add the bitters. Serve immediately.

THE STONE FENCE

Serves 1

Ingredients

1½ measures bourbon
2 dashes Angostura bitters
ice
sparkling cider
sprig of mint, bruised,
to decorate

1. Add the bourbon and bitters to a chilled highball glass filled with ice.

2. Top with cider.

3. Dress with the mint sprig and serve immediately.

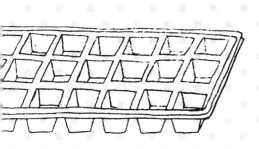

APPLE FIZZ

Serves 1

Ingredients

125 ml/4 fl oz sparkling cider
or apple juice
1 measure Calvados
juice of ½ lemon
1 tbsp egg white
generous pinch sugar
ice
slices of lemon and apple,
to decorate

1. Shake the first five ingredients together over the ice.

2. Pour immediately into a glass.

3. Dress with a slice of lemon and apple and serve immediately.

APPLE BREEZE

Serves 1

Ingredients

1 measure coconut rum

ice

sparkling cider

slice of apple, to decorate

1. Add the liqueur to a chilled highball glass half-filled with ice.

2. Top with the cider.

3. Dress the glass with the apple slice and serve immediately.

BLOOD ON THE TRACKS

Serves 1

Ingredients

½ measure Campari bitters

ice

2½ measures blood orange juice

sparkling water

slice of orange and sprig of mint, to decorate

1. Pour the bitters into a chilled highball glass filled with ice.

2. Add the juice. Do not stir.

3. Top up with sparkling water.

4. Dress with the orange slice and mint and serve immediately.

RASPBERRY LEMONADE

Serves 4

Ingredients

2 lemons

115 g/4 oz icing sugar

115 g/4 oz raspberries

few drops vanilla extract

cracked ice cubes

sparkling water

fresh mint sprigs, to decorate

1. Cut the ends off the lemons, then scoop out and chop the flesh.

2. Put the lemon flesh in a blender with the sugar, raspberries, vanilla extract and 4–6 cracked ice cubes and blend for 2–3 minutes.

3. Half fill four highball glasses with cracked ice and strain in the blended mixture.

4. Top up with sparkling water and decorate with the mint sprigs. Serve immediately.

COOL COLLINS

Serves 1

Ingredients

6 fresh mint leaves, plus extra to decorate

1 tsp caster sugar

2 measures lemon juice

cracked ice cubes

sparkling water

lemon slice, to decorate

1. Put the mint leaves into a chilled Collins glass.

2. Add the sugar and lemon juice.

3. Crush the mint leaves, then stir until the sugar has dissolved.

4. Fill the glass with cracked ice cubes and top up with sparkling water.

5. Stir gently and decorate with the fresh mint and lemon slice. Serve immediately.

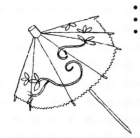

HEAVENLY DAYS

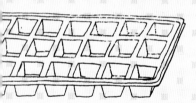

Serves 1

Ingredients

cracked ice
2 measures hazelnut syrup
2 measures lemon juice
1 tsp grenadine
sparkling water

1. Put 4–6 cracked ice cubes into a cocktail shaker.

2. Pour over the hazelnut syrup, lemon juice and grenadine and shake vigorously until well frosted.

3. Half fill a tumbler with cracked ice and strain the cocktail over.

4. Top up with sparkling water and stir gently.

5. Serve immediately.

Top tip
This is the perfect headache-free cocktail to indulge in on a hot summer's day.

SUMMER PUNCH

Serves 8

Ingredients

700 ml/1¼ pints rosé wine, chilled

1 tbsp honey

150 ml/5 fl oz brandy (optional)

115 g/4 oz mixed summer berries, such as raspberries, blueberries and strawberries

3-4 fresh mint sprigs, plus extra to garnish

600 ml/1 pint sparkling water, chilled

ice cubes

1. Pour the wine into a punch bowl or large glass serving bowl. Add the honey and stir well. Add the brandy, if using.

2. Cut any large berries into bite-sized pieces and place all the berries and mint sprigs into the wine.

3. Leave to stand for 15 minutes, then add the sparkling water and ice cubes. Ladle the punch into glasses or punch cups ensuring each has an ice cube and a few pieces of fruit. Serve immediately, decorated with mint sprigs.

EL DIABLO

Serves 1

Ingredients

1 measure tequila
½ measure fresh lime juice
½ measure crème de cassis
cracked ice
ginger ale
slice of lime, to decorate

1. Add the tequila, juice and cassis to a shaker filled with ice. Shake well.

2. Strain into a chilled highball glass filled with ice.

3. Top up with ginger ale. Dress the glass with the lime. Serve immediately.

EL TORO

Serves 1

Ingredients

2 measures tequila
1 measure coffee liqueur
1 measure single cream
cracked ice

1. Pour the tequila, coffee liqueur and cream into a shaker filled with ice.

2. Shake well and strain into a chilled martini glass. Serve immediately.

HIGH VOLTAGE

Serves 1

Ingredients

2 measures tequila

1 measure peach schnapps

½ measure fresh lime juice

cracked ice

fresh peach slice, peeled,
to decorate

1. Pour the tequila, schnapps and juice into a shaker filled with ice.

2. Shake well and strain into a chilled martini glass.

3. Dress the glass with the peach slice and serve immediately.

SILK STOCKINGS

Serves 1

Ingredients

1½ measures tequila

½ measure raspberry liqueur

½ measure crème de cacao

1 measure double cream

cracked ice

fresh raspberries, to decorate

1. Pour the tequila, liqueurs and cream into a shaker filled with ice.

2. Shake well and strain into a chilled martini glass.

3. Dress the glass with raspberries on a cocktail stick. Serve immediately.

TEQUILA SLAMMER

Serves 1

Ingredients

1 measure silver tequila,
chilled
juice of ½ lemon
sparkling wine, chilled

1. Put the tequila into a chilled glass.

2. Add the lemon juice.

3. Top up with sparkling wine.

4. Cover the glass with your hand and slam to mix.

5. Serve immediately.

126

TEQUILA SUNRISE

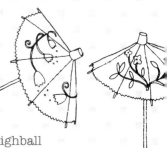

Serves 1

Ingredients

4–6 cracked ice cubes
2 measures silver tequila
orange juice
1 measure grenadine
orange slice and cocktail
cherry, to decorate

1. Put the cracked ice cubes into a chilled highball glass. Pour over the tequila.

2. Top up with orange juice.

3. Stir well to mix.

4. Slowly pour over the grenadine. Decorate with the orange slice and cocktail cherry.

5. Serve immediately.

BLACK RUSSIAN

Serves 1

Ingredients

2 measures vodka

1 measure coffee liqueur

cracked ice cubes

1. Pour the vodka and liqueur over cracked ice cubes in a chilled lowball glass.

2. Stir to mix and serve immediately.

JEALOUSY

Serves 1

Ingredients

1 tsp crème de menthe

1-2 tbsp double cream

2 measures coffee liqueur or chocolate liqueur

chocolate matchsticks, to serve

1. Gently beat the crème de menthe into the cream until thick.

2. Pour the coffee liqueur into a chilled shot glass and carefully spoon over the whipped flavoured cream.

3. Serve immediately with the chocolate matchsticks.

BANANA SLIP

Serves 1

Ingredients

1 measure crème de banane, chilled

1 measure Irish cream liqueur, chilled

1. Pour the chilled crème de banane into a chilled shot glass.

2. With a steady hand, gently pour in the chilled cream liqueur to make a second layer. Serve immediately.

BLOODY BRAIN

Serves 1

Ingredients

1 measure peach schnapps, chilled

1 tsp Irish cream liqueur, chilled

½ tsp grenadine, chilled

1. Pour the peach schnapps into a shot glass, then carefully pour the cream liqueur on top.

2. Finally, pour in the grenadine and serve immediately.

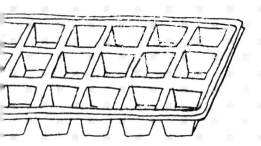

BVD

Serves 1

Ingredients

1 measure brandy
1 measure dry vermouth
1 measure Dubonnet
cracked ice

1. Pour the brandy, dry vermouth and Dubonnet over cracked ice in a mixing glass.

2. Stir to mix and strain into a chilled cocktail glass. Serve immediately.

Fact

A number of cocktails are known simply by their initials. In this classic recipe BVD stands for brandy, vermouth and Dubonnet.

SCS

Serves 1

Ingredients

2 measures sloe gin

orange juice

cracked ice cubes

orange slice, to decorate

1. Shake the sloe gin and orange juice over cracked ice until well frosted and pour into a chilled glass.

2. Dress with the orange slice and serve immediately.

AFRICAN MINT

Serves 1

Ingredients

¾ measure crème de menthe, chilled

¾ measure Amarula, chilled

1. Pour the crème de menthe into a chilled shot glass, reserving a few drops.

2. Pour the Amarula slowly over the back of a spoon to create a second layer.

3. Drizzle the remaining drops of crème de menthe over the creamy liqueur to finish. Serve immediately.

ZANDER

Serves 1

Ingredients

cracked ice cubes

1 measure Sambuca

1 measure orange juice

dash lemon juice

bitter lemon

1. Fill a chilled glass with cracked ice.

2. Shake the Sambuca, orange juice and lemon juice vigorously over cracked ice until well frosted.

3. Strain into the glass and top up with bitter lemon. Serve immediately.

FRENCH KISS

Serves 1

Ingredients

4-6 cracked ice cubes

2 measures bourbon

1 measure apricot liqueur

2 tsp grenadine

1 tsp lemon juice

1. Put the cracked ice cubes into a cocktail shaker.

2. Pour over the liquid ingredients and shake vigorously until well frosted.

3. Strain into a chilled cocktail glass and serve immediately.

QUEEN OF MEMPHIS

Serves 1

Ingredients

4-6 cracked ice cubes

2 measures bourbon

1 measure Midori

1 measure peach juice

dash of maraschino liqueur

melon wedge, to decorate

1. Put the cracked ice cubes into a cocktail shaker.

2. Pour over the bourbon, Midori, peach juice and maraschino and shake vigorously until well frosted.

3. Strain into a chilled cocktail glass. Decorate with the melon wedge and serve immediately.

RATTLESNAKE

Serves 1

Ingredients

1 measure dark crème de cacao, chilled

1 measure Irish cream liqueur, chilled

1 measure Kahlúa, chilled

1. Pour the chilled crème de cacao into a shot glass.

2. With a steady hand, gently pour in the chilled cream liqueur over the back of a spoon to make a second layer.

3. Pour in the chilled Kahlúa to make a third layer. Do not stir. Serve immediately.

Fact
This potent layered drink is named for its resemblance to the venomous snake's striped tail.

AFTER FIVE

Serves 1

Ingredients

½ measure peppermint schnapps, chilled

1 measure Kahlúa, chilled

1 tbsp Irish cream liqueur

1. Pour the peppermint schnapps into a chilled shot glass.

2. Carefully pour the Kahlúa over the back of a spoon to make a second layer.

3. Finally, float the cream liqueur on top. Serve immediately.

MELLOW MULE

Serves 1

Ingredients

4–6 cracked ice cubes

2 measures white rum

1 measure dark rum

1 measure golden rum

1 measure falernum
(wine-based ginger syrup)

1 measure lime juice

ginger beer

pineapple wedges and stem
ginger, to decorate

1. Put the cracked ice cubes into a cocktail shaker.

2. Pour over the white rum, dark rum, golden rum, falernum and lime juice and shake vigorously until well frosted.

3. Strain the cocktail into a tall, chilled tumbler.

4. Top up with ginger beer and decorate with the pineapple wedges and ginger. Serve immediately.

JOSIAH'S BAY FLOAT

Serves 2

Ingredients

4–6 cracked ice cubes

2 measures golden rum

1 measure Galliano

2 measures pineapple juice

1 measure lime juice

4 tsp sugar syrup

scooped-out pineapple shell,
to serve

champagne

lime slices, lemon slices and
cocktail cherries, to decorate

1. Put the cracked ice cubes into a cocktail shaker.

2. Pour over the rum, Galliano, pineapple juice, lime juice and sugar syrup and shake vigorously until well frosted.

3. Strain into the pineapple shell.

4. Top up with champagne and decorate with the lime and lemon slices and cocktail cherries. Serve immediately.

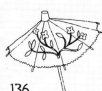

MINTED DIAMONDS

Serves 1

Ingredients

1 tsp green crème de menthe

1 tbsp iced water

1 measure white crème de menthe

2 measures apple or pear schnapps

1. Mix the green crème de menthe with the water. Pour into an ice cube tray and freeze.

2. Stir the white crème de menthe and apple or pear schnapps over ice until well frosted.

3. Strain the cocktail into a chilled glass and add the mint ice cubes. Drink when the ice cubes begin to melt.

BANANA DAIQUIRI

Serves 1

Ingredients

2 measures white rum, chilled

½ measure triple sec, chilled

½ measure lime juice

½ measure single cream, chilled

1 tsp sugar syrup

¼ banana, peeled and sliced

lime slice, to decorate

1. Put all the liquid ingredients into a blender.

2. Add the banana and blend until smooth.

3. Pour, without straining, into a chilled tumbler.

4. Decorate with the lime slice and serve immediately.

CAIPIRINHA

Serves 1

Ingredients

6 lime wedges
2 tsp granulated sugar
3 measures cachaça
4-6 cracked ice cubes

1. Put the lime wedges in a chilled lowball glass.

2. Add the sugar.

3. Muddle the lime wedges, then pour over the cachaça.

4. Fill the glass with the cracked ice and stir well.

5. Serve immediately.

BOURBON MILK PUNCH

Serves 1

Ingredients

4-6 cracked ice cubes
2 measures bourbon
3 measures milk
dash of vanilla extract
1 tsp clear honey
freshly grated nutmeg,
to decorate

1. Put the cracked ice cubes into a cocktail shaker.

2. Pour over the bourbon, milk and vanilla extract.

3. Add the honey and shake until well frosted.

4. Strain into a chilled tumbler. Sprinkle over the grated nutmeg.

5. Serve immediately.

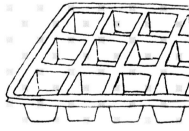

CHERRYCOLA

Serves 1

Ingredients

6-8 ice cubes, cracked

2 measures cherry brandy

1 measure lemon juice

cola

lemon slice

1. Half fill a chilled highball glass or lowball glass with the cracked ice.

2. Pour the cherry brandy and lemon juice over the ice.

3. Top up with cola, stir gently and decorate with a slice of lemon. Serve immediately.

BLUE LAGOON

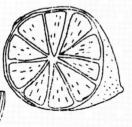

Serves 1

Ingredients

1 measure blue curaçao

1 measure vodka

dash lemon juice

lemonade

1. Pour the curaçao into a chilled cocktail glass, followed by the vodka.

2. Add the lemon juice and top up with lemonade. Serve immediately.

TORNADO

Serves 1

Ingredients

1 measure peach or other favourite schnapps, frozen

1 measure black sambuca, frozen

1. Pour the schnapps into a chilled shot glass.

2. Gently pour in the sambuca over the back of a spoon.

3. Leave to stand for a few minutes to settle and separate before drinking

WHITE DIAMOND FRAPPÉ

Serves 1

Ingredients

¼ measure peppermint schnapps

¼ measure white crème de cacao

¼ measure anise liqueur

¼ measure lemon juice

crushed ice

1. Shake the peppermint schnapps, white crème de cacao, anise liqueur and lemon juice over some of the crushed ice until frosted.

2. Strain into a chilled cocktail glass and add a small extra spoonful of crushed ice. Serve immediately.

B-52

Serves 1

Ingredients

1 measure chilled dark crème de cacao

1 measure chilled Irish cream liqueur

1 measure chilled Grand Marnier

1. Pour the crème de cacao into a shot glass.

2. With a steady hand, gently pour in the cream liqueur to make a second layer.

3. Gently pour in the Grand Marnier.

4. Cover with your hand and slam to mix, or alternatively serve with layers intact.

5. Serve immediately.

TRICOLOUR

Serves 1

Ingredients

1 measure chilled red maraschino liqueur

1 measure chilled crème de menthe

1 measure chilled Irish cream liqueur

fresh mint leaf, to decorate

1. Pour the maraschino into a chilled shot glass.

2. Gently pour in the crème de menthe to make a second layer.

3. Gently pour in the cream liqueur.

4. Decorate with the mint leaf.

5. Serve immediately.

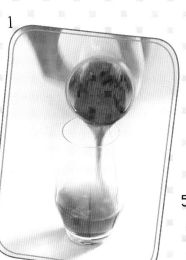

SHADY LADY

Serves 1

Ingredients

3 measures tequila

1 measure apple brandy

1 measure cranberry juice

dash of lime juice

1. Shake the tequila, apple brandy, cranberry juice and a dash of lime juice over ice cubes until well frosted.

2. Strain into a chilled cocktail glass and serve immediately.

PEACH FLOYD

Serves 1

Ingredients

1 measure peach schnapps, chilled

1 measure vodka, chilled

1 measure white cranberry and peach juice, chilled

1 measure cranberry juice, chilled

cracked ice cubes

1. Stir all the liquid ingredients together over cracked ice.

2. Pour into a chilled shot glass and serve immediately.

CLIMAX

Serves 1

Ingredients

1 measure Irish cream liqueur

1 measure almond-flavoured liqueur

1 measure coffee liqueur

1 measure single cream

cracked ice and ice cubes

1. Pour the liqueurs and cream into a cocktail shaker filled with cracked ice.

2. Shake well and strain into a chilled old-fashioned glass filled with ice cubes. Serve immediately.

MOO MOO

Serves 1

Ingredients

1 measure Irish cream liqueur

1 measure crème de cacao

3 measures single cream

cracked ice and ice cubes

ground cinnamon, to decorate

1. Pour the liqueurs and cream into a cocktail shaker filled with cracked ice.

2. Shake well and strain into a chilled highball glass filled with ice cubes.

3. Sprinkle a little cinnamon on top and serve immediately

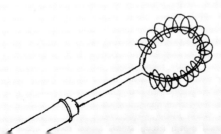

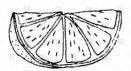

SANGRIA

Serves 6

Ingredients

juice of 1 orange
juice of 1 lemon
2 tbsp icing sugar
cracked ice cubes
1 orange, thinly sliced
1 lemon, thinly sliced
1 bottle chilled red wine
lemonade, to taste

1. Put the orange juice and lemon juice in a large jug. Stir.

2. Add the sugar and stir. When the sugar has dissolved, add the ice cubes, sliced fruit and wine and marinate for 1 hour.

3. Add lemonade to taste, then top up with cracked ice. Serve immediately.

Top tip
You can vary the combination of fruit according to taste and availability.

PINK SQUIRREL

Serves 1

Ingredients

2 measures dark crème de cacao

1 measure crème de noyau

1 measure single cream

cracked ice

1. Pour the crème de cacao, crème de noyau and single cream over the cracked ice and shake vigorously until well frosted.

2. Strain into a chilled cocktail glass and serve immediately.

FIRELIGHTER

Serves 1

Ingredients

1 measure absinthe, iced

1 measure lime cordial, iced

cracked ice cubes

1. Shake the absinthe and lime cordial vigorously over cracked ice until well frosted.

2. Strain into a chilled shot glass and serve immediately.

AMARETTO COFFEE

Serves 1

Ingredients

1½ measures amaretto

sugar

freshly made strong black coffee

1-2 tbsp double cream

1. Put the amaretto into a warmed heatproof glass and add sugar to taste.

2. Pour in the coffee and stir.

3. When the sugar has completely dissolved, pour in the cream very slowly over the back of a spoon so that it floats on top.

4. Don't stir – drink the coffee through the cream.

AMARETTO STINGER

Serves 1

Ingredients

2 measures amaretto

1 measure white crème de menthe

cracked ice cubes

1. Shake the amaretto and white crème de menthe vigorously over cracked ice until well frosted.

2. Strain into a chilled lowball glass and serve immediately.

MUDSLIDE

Serves 1

Ingredients

1½ measures Kahlúa

1½ measures Irish cream liqueur

1½ measures vodka

cracked ice cubes

1. Shake the Kahlúa, cream liqueur and vodka vigorously over cracked ice until well frosted.

2. Strain into a chilled glass and serve immediately.

IRISH STINGER

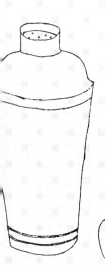

Serves 1

Ingredients

1 measure Irish cream liqueur

1 measure white crème de menthe

cracked ice cubes

1. Shake the cream liqueur and white crème de menthe vigorously over cracked ice until well frosted.

2. Strain into a chilled shot or lowball glass.

Top tip
Substitute the Irish cream liqueur for 2 measures of brandy to make the classic Stinger cocktail instead.

WHITE COSMOPOLITAN

Serves 1

Ingredients

1½ measures limoncello

½ measure Cointreau

1 measure white cranberry
and grape juice

cracked ice cubes

dash orange bitters

cranberries, to decorate

1. Shake the limoncello, Cointreau and white cranberry and grape juice over cracked ice until frosted.

2. Strain into a chilled cocktail glass.

3. Add the bitters and dress with the cranberries and serve immediately

CHOCOLATE MARTINI

Serves 1

Ingredients

slice of orange

cocoa powder

2 measures vodka

¼ measure crème de cacao

2 dashes orange flower water

ice cubes

twist of orange peel

1. Moisten the rim of a cocktail glass with an orange slice. Dip in cocoa powder and set aside.

2. Shake the vodka, crème de cacao and orange flower water over ice cubes until really well frosted.

3. Strain into the cocktail glass and decorate with a twist of orange peel. Serve immediately

ALABAMA SLAMMER

Serves 1

Ingredients

1 measure Southern Comfort

1 measure amaretto

1 measure sloe gin

cracked ice

½ tsp lemon juice

1. Pour the Southern Comfort, amaretto and sloe gin over cracked ice in a mixing glass and stir.

2. Strain into a shot glass and add the lemon juice. Cover with your hand, slam on the table and drink immediately.

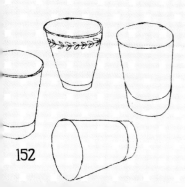

TOFFEE SPLIT

Serves 1

Ingredients

crushed ice

2 measures Drambuie

1 measure toffee liqueur, iced

1. Fill a shot glass with crushed ice.

2. Pour the Drambuie over the ice, then pour in the toffee liqueur over the back of a spoon to make a layer on top. Serve immediately.

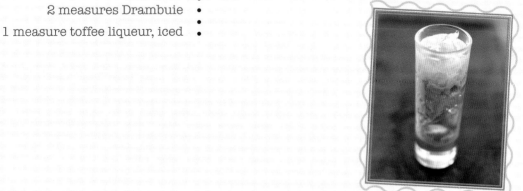

VOODOO

Serves 1

Ingredients

½ measure Kahlúa, chilled

½ measure Malibu, chilled

½ measure butterscotch schnapps, chilled

1 measure milk, chilled

1. Pour the Kahlúa, Malibu, butterscotch schnapps and milk into a chilled shot glass and stir well. Serve immediately.

NAPOLEON'S NIGHTCAP

Serves 1

Ingredients

1¼ measures cognac

1 measure dark crème de cacao

¼ measure crème de banane

cracked ice cubes

1 tbsp cream

1. Stir the cognac, crème de cacao and crème de banane in a mixing glass with cracked ice.

2. Strain into a chilled cocktail glass and float the cream on top. Serve immediately.

Fact
Instead of hot chocolate at bedtime, Napoleon apparently knocked back a chocolate laced brandy with a hint of banana.

IRISH COFFEE

Serves 1

Ingredients

2 measures Irish whiskey

sugar

freshly made strong
black coffee

2 measures double cream

1. Put the whiskey into a warmed heatproof glass and add sugar to taste.

2. Pour in the coffee and stir.

3. When the sugar has completely dissolved, pour in the cream very slowly over the back of a spoon so that it floats on top.

4. Don't stir – drink the coffee through the cream.

MINI COLADA

Serves 1

Ingredients

cracked ice cubes
6 measures milk
3 measures coconut cream
4 measures pineapple juice

To decorate

pineapple chunk
pineapple leaf
cocktail cherry

1. Put 4–6 cracked ice cubes into a cocktail shaker.

2. Pour over the milk and coconut cream.

3. Add the pineapple juice and shake vigorously until well frosted.

4. Half fill a highball glass with cracked ice, strain the cocktail into it and decorate with the pineapple chunk, pineapple leaf and cherry. Serve immediately.

MAIDENLY MIMOSA

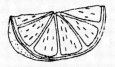

Serves 2

Ingredients

175 ml/6 fl oz orange juice
175 ml/6 fl oz sparkling white grape juice
orange slices, to decorate

1. Chill two champagne flutes.

2. Divide the orange juice between the flutes and top up with the sparkling grape juice.

3. Decorate with the orange slices and serve immediately.

BRIGHT GREEN COOLER

Serves 1

Ingredients

cracked ice cubes

3 measures pineapple juice

2 measures lime juice

1 measure green peppermint syrup

ginger ale

cucumber strip and lime slice, to decorate

1. Put 4–6 cracked ice cubes into a cocktail shaker.

2. Pour over the pineapple juice, lime juice and peppermint syrup and shake vigorously until well frosted.

3. Half fill a chilled highball glass with cracked ice and strain the cocktail over it.

4. Top up with ginger ale and decorate with the cucumber strip and lime slice. Serve immediately.

SHIRLEY TEMPLE

Serves 1

Ingredients

cracked ice cubes

2 measures lemon juice

½ measure grenadine

½ measure sugar syrup

ginger ale

orange slice, to decorate

1. Put 4–6 cracked ice cubes into a cocktail shaker.

2. Pour over the lemon juice, grenadine and sugar syrup and shake vigorously until well frosted.

3. Half fill a chilled highball glass with cracked ice, then strain the cocktail over it.

4. Top up with ginger ale and decorate with the orange slice. Serve immediately.

PROHIBITION PUNCH

Serves 6

Ingredients

850 ml/1½ pints apple juice

350 ml/12 fl oz lemon juice

125 ml/4 fl oz sugar syrup

cracked ice cubes

2¼ litres/4 pints ginger ale

orange slices, to decorate

1. Pour the apple juice into a large jug.

2. Add the lemon juice and sugar syrup and a handful of cracked ice cubes.

3. Add the ginger ale and stir gently to mix. Pour into chilled lowball glasses and decorate with the orange slices. Serve immediately.

Top tip
This is the perfect punch to serve to children at a summer party.

RED APPLE SUNSET

Serves 1

Ingredients

2 measures apple juice

2 measures grapefruit juice

dash of grenadine

ice cubes

1. Shake the apple juice, grapefruit juice and a dash of grenadine over ice cubes until well frosted.

2. Strain into a chilled cocktail glass and serve immediately.

FAUX KIR ROYALE

Serves 1

Ingredients

4-6 cracked ice cubes

1½ measures raspberry syrup

sparkling apple juice, chilled

1. Put the cracked ice cubes into a mixing glass. Pour over the raspberry syrup.

2. Stir well to mix and strain into a chilled wine glass.

3. Top up with sparkling apple juice and stir.

4. Serve immediately.

BABY BELLINI

Serves 1

Ingredients

2 measures peach juice

1 measure lemon juice

sparkling apple juice

1. Pour the peach juice and lemon juice into a chilled champagne flute and stir well.

2. Top up with sparkling apple juice and stir again. Serve immediately.

RANCH GIRL

Serves 1

Ingredients

1 measure lime juice

1 measure barbecue sauce

Worcestershire sauce

hot pepper sauce

tomato juice

lime slices and 1 pickled jalapeño chilli, to decorate

1. Shake the lime juice, barbecue sauce and dashes of Worcestershire sauce and hot pepper sauce over ice cubes until well frosted.

2. Pour into a chilled highball glass, top up with tomato juice and stir.

3. Dress with a couple of slices of lime and a pickled jalapeño chilli. Serve immediately.

BITE OF THE APPLE

Serves 1

Ingredients

crushed ice

5 measures apple juice

1 measure lime juice

½ tsp orgeat syrup

1 tbsp apple sauce or apple purée

ground cinnamon

1. Whizz the crushed ice in a blender with the apple juice, lime juice, orgeat syrup and apple sauce until smooth.

2. Pour into a chilled lowball glass and sprinkle with cinnamon. Serve immediately.

VIRGIN MARY

Serves 1

Ingredients

4-6 cracked ice cubes
3 measures tomato juice
1 measure lemon juice
2 dashes Worcestershire sauce
1 dash hot pepper sauce
pinch celery salt
pepper
lemon wedge and celery stick,
to decorate

1. Put the cracked ice cubes into a cocktail shaker. Pour over the tomato juice.

2. Add the lemon juice.

3. Pour in the Worcestershire sauce and hot pepper sauce. Shake vigorously until well frosted.

4. Season to taste with the celery salt and pepper, strain into a chilled glass and decorate with the lemon wedge and celery stick.

5. Serve immediately.

SANGRÍA SECA

Serves 6

Ingredients

475 ml/16 fl oz tomato juice

225 ml/8 fl oz orange juice

3 measures lime juice

½ measure hot pepper sauce

2 tsp Worcestershire sauce

1 jalapeño chilli, deseeded and
finely chopped

celery salt

white pepper (preferably
freshly ground)

cracked ice

1. Pour the tomato juice, orange juice, lime juice, hot pepper sauce and Worcestershire sauce into a jug.

2. Add the chopped chilli and season to taste with the celery salt and white pepper.

3. Stir well, cover and chill in the refrigerator for at least an hour.

4. To serve, half fill chilled highball glasses with cracked ice and strain the cocktail over it.

5. Serve immediately.

2

1

5

KNICKS VICTORY COOLER

Serves 1

Ingredients

cracked ice

2 measures apricot juice

raspberry juice

orange peel twist and a few
raspberries, to decorate

1. Half fill a chilled highball glass with the
cracked ice.

2. Pour the apricot juice over the ice, top up with
raspberry juice and stir gently.

3. Decorate with an
orange peel twist and
fresh raspberries.
Serve immediately.

NEW ENGLAND PARTY

Serves 2

Ingredients

crushed ice

dash of hot pepper sauce

dash of Worcestershire sauce

1 tsp lemon juice

1 medium carrot, chopped

2 celery sticks, chopped

300 ml/10 fl oz tomato juice

150 ml/5 fl oz clam juice

salt and freshly ground
black pepper

celery sticks, to decorate

1. Put all the ingredients, except the seasoning and
celery stick, into a blender and blend until smooth.

2. Transfer to a jug, cover and chill in the
refrigerator for about an hour.

3. Pour into two chilled highball glasses and season
to taste.

4. Dress with a celery
stick and serve
immediately.

FRUIT COOLER

Serves 2

Ingredients

225 ml/8 fl oz orange juice

125 ml/4 fl oz natural yogurt

2 eggs

2 bananas, sliced and frozen

fresh banana slices

1. Pour the orange juice and yogurt into a food processor and process gently until combined.

2. Add the eggs and frozen bananas and process until smooth.

3. Pour the mixture into highball or hurricane glasses and decorate the rims with slices of fresh banana. Serve immediately.

CITRUS FIZZ

Serves 1

Ingredients

2 measures fresh orange juice, chilled

icing sugar

squeeze lime juice

few drops Angostura bitters

2-3 measures sparkling water, chilled

1. Rub the rim of a flute with orange or lime juice and dip into the icing sugar.

2. Stir the rest of the juices together with the bitters and then pour into the glass.

3. Add sparkling water to taste and serve immediately.

MANGO LASSI

Serves 2

Ingredients

225 ml/8 fl oz milk

125 ml/4 fl oz natural yogurt

1 tbsp rosewater

3 tbsp honey

1 ripe mango, peeled and diced

4-6 ice cubes

rose petals, to decorate
(optional)

1. Pour the milk and yogurt into a blender and process until combined.

2. Add the rosewater and honey and process until blended.

3. Add the mango and ice cubes and blend until smooth.

4. Pour into two chilled glasses and decorate with the rose petals, if using.

5. Serve immediately.

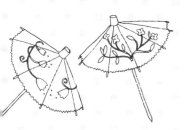

COCONUT CREAM

Serves 2

Ingredients

350 ml/12 fl oz pineapple juice

90ml/3¼ fl oz coconut milk

150 g/5½ oz vanilla ice cream

140 g/5 oz frozen pineapple chunks

grated fresh coconut, to decorate

1. Pour the pineapple juice and coconut milk into a blender.

2. Add the ice cream and process until smooth.

3. Add the pineapple chunks and process until smooth.

4. Divide between two chilled glasses and decorate with the grated coconut.

5. Serve immediately.

2

1

5

COCOBERRY

Serves 1

Ingredients

90 g/3¼ oz raspberries

crushed ice

1 measure coconut cream

150 ml/5 fl oz pineapple juice

pineapple wedge

a few raspberries

1. Rub the raspberries through a strainer with the back of a spoon and transfer the purée to a blender.

2. Add the crushed ice, coconut cream and pineapple juice and blend until smooth, then pour the mixture, without straining, into a chilled lowball glass.

3. Dress with a pineapple wedge and fresh raspberries. Serve immediately.

COCOBELLE

Serves 1

Ingredients

3 measures cold milk

1 measure coconut cream

2 scoops vanilla ice cream

3–4 ice cubes

dash grenadine

desiccated coconut, toasted, to decorate

1. Blend the first four ingredients in a blender until slushy.

2. Chill a tall glass and gently dribble a few splashes of grenadine down the insides.

3. Pour in the slush slowly and top with the toasted coconut. Serve immediately.

SLUSH PUPPY

Serves 1

Ingredients

juice of 1 lemon or ½ pink grapefruit

30 ml/2 tbsp grenadine

ice cubes

few strips of lemon peel

2–3 tsp raspberry syrup

soda water

cherry, to decorate

1. Pour the lemon juice and grenadine into a chilled tall glass with ice.

2. Add the lemon peel, syrup and soda water to taste. Decorate with a cherry and serve immediately.

THAI FRUIT COCKTAIL

Serves 1

Ingredients

50 ml/2 fl oz pineapple juice

50 ml/2 fl oz orange juice

1 tbsp lime juice

50 ml/2 fl oz passion fruit juice

100 ml/3½ fl oz guava juice

crushed ice

flower, to decorate

1. Shake the ingredients over ice in a cocktail shaker.

2. Pour into a chilled long glass and finish with a flower. Serve immediately.

APPLE PIE CREAM

Serves 1

Ingredients

4-6 cracked ice cubes

4 measures apple juice

1 small scoop vanilla ice cream

soda water

cinnamon sugar and apple slice, to decorate

1. Put the cracked ice cubes into a blender and add the apple juice and ice cream.

2. Blend for 10-15 seconds until frothy and frosted. Pour into a glass and top up with soda water.

3. Sprinkle over the cinnamon sugar and decorate with an apple slice. Serve immediately.

Top tip

For an alcoholic version of this sweet treat, use apple cider instead of the apple juice.

PEACHY CREAM

Serves 1

Ingredients

3 measures peach juice, chilled

2 measures single cream

cracked ice

1. Pour the peach juice and cream together over ice cubes and shake vigorously until well frosted.

2. Half fill a chilled highball glass or lowball glass with cracked ice and strain the cocktail over it. Serve immediately.

GINGER FIZZ

Serves 1

Ingredients

ginger ale

fresh mint sprigs, plus extra to decorate

cracked ice

fresh raspberries, to decorate

1. Put 2 measures of ginger ale into a blender, add a few mint sprigs and blend together.

2. Strain into a chilled highball glass two-thirds filled with cracked ice and top up with more ginger ale.

3. Decorate with raspberries and the mint sprig. Serve immediately.

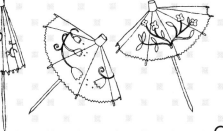

SOBER SUNDAY

Serves 1

Ingredients

50 ml/2 fl oz grenadine

50 ml/2 fl oz fresh lemon or lime juice

ice cubes

lemonade

fresh lemon or lime slices, to decorate

1. Pour the grenadine and fruit juice into an ice-filled highball glass.

2. Top up with lemonade and finish with slices of lemon and lime. Serve immediately.

LONG BOAT

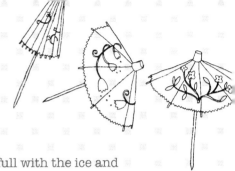

Serves 1

Ingredients

ice cubes

1 measure lime cordial

ginger beer

lime wedge and mint sprig,
to decorate

1. Fill a chilled glass two-thirds full with the ice and pour in the lime cordial.

2. Top up with ginger beer and stir gently.

3. Decorate with the lime wedge and the mint sprig. Serve immediately.

CRANBERRY ENERGIZER

Serves 2

Ingredients

300 ml/10 fl oz cranberry juice

125 ml/4 fl oz orange juice

55 g/2 oz fresh raspberries

1 tbsp lemon juice

fresh orange slices, to decorate

1. Pour the cranberry juice and orange juice into a blender and blend gently until combined.

2. Add the raspberries and lemon juice and blend until smooth.

3. Strain into glasses and dress with the slices of orange. Serve immediately.

THE GUNNER

Serves 1

Ingredients

4–6 ice cubes

50 ml/2 fl oz lime juice

2–3 dashes of Angostura bitters or to taste

200 ml/7 fl oz ginger beer

200 ml/7 fl oz lemonade

1. Mix all the ingredients together in a long glass.

2. Taste and add more Angostura bitters if you wish. Serve immediately.

Top tip
The Gunner is renowned for being light and refreshing, perfect for a hot summer evening.

PEAR & RASPBERRY DELIGHT

Serves 2

Ingredients

2 large ripe Anjou pears, peeled, cored and chopped

140 g/5 oz frozen raspberries

175 ml/6 fl oz ice-cold water

honey, to taste

raspberries, to decorate

1. Put the pears into a blender with the raspberries and water and blend until smooth.

2. Taste and sweeten with honey if the raspberries are a little sharp.

3. Strain into glasses and decorate with the raspberries. Serve immediately.

STRAWBERRY COLADA

Serves 2

Ingredients

450 g/1 lb strawberries
125 ml/4 fl oz coconut cream
600 ml/1 pint chilled
pineapple juice

1. Reserve four strawberries to decorate. Halve the remainder and place in the blender.

2. Add the coconut cream and pineapple juice and blend until smooth, then pour into chilled glasses and dress with the reserved strawberries. Serve immediately.

ST. CLEMENTS

Serves 2

Ingredients

ice cubes
2 measures orange juice
2 measures bitter lemon
orange and lemon slices,
to decorate

1. Put the ice cubes into a chilled tumbler. Pour in the orange juice and bitter lemon.

2. Stir gently and dress with the slices of orange and lemon. Serve immediately.

BANANA COFFEE BREAK

Serves 2

Ingredients

300 ml/10 fl oz milk

4 tbsp instant coffee powder

140 g/5 oz vanilla ice cream

2 bananas, sliced and frozen
plus extra slices, to decorate

brown sugar to taste

1. Pour the milk into a food processor, add the coffee powder and process gently until combined. Add half the vanilla ice cream and process gently, then add the remaining ice cream and process until well combined.

2. When thoroughly blended, add the bananas and sugar to taste and process until smooth.

3. Pour into highball glasses and serve dressed with a few slices of banana. Serve immediately.

COCO COLADA

Serves 1

Ingredients

4 measures pineapple juice

2 measures coconut cream

cup of crushed ice

pineapple chunk and cherry,
to decorate

1. Pour the juice and coconut cream into a blender, and add the ice.

2. Blend until combined and slushy and pour into a chilled glass.

3. Dress the glass with the pineapple and cherry on a stick. Serve immediately.

179

SOFT SANGRIA

Serves 10

Ingredients

1.5 litres/2¾ pints red
grape juice

300 ml/10 fl oz orange juice

75 ml/2½ fl oz cranberry juice

50 ml/2 fl oz lemon juice

50 ml/2 fl oz lime juice

100 ml/3½ fl oz sugar syrup

ice cubes

lemon, orange and lime slices,
to decorate

1. Put the grape juice, orange juice, cranberry juice, lemon juice, lime juice and sugar syrup into a chilled punch bowl and stir well.

2. Add the ice and decorate with the slices of lemon, orange and lime.

Top tip

This is a non-alcoholic version of the Spanish classic. Make sure all ingredients are well chilled before combining.

SUNRISE

Serves 1

Ingredients

cracked ice
2 measures orange juice
1 measure lemon juice
1 measure grenadine
sparkling mineral water

1. Put the cracked ice into a chilled highball glass and pour the orange juice, lemon juice and grenadine over it.

2. Stir together well and top up with sparkling mineral water. Serve immediately.

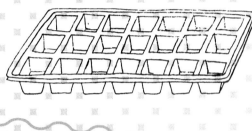

POM POM

Serves 1

Ingredients

juice of ½ lemon

1 egg white

1 dash of grenadine

crushed ice

lemonade

lemon slice,
to decorate

1. Shake the lemon juice, egg white and grenadine together and strain over crushed ice in a tall glass.

2. Top up with lemonade and dress with a lemon slice on the rim of the glass. Serve immediately.

PERKY PINEAPPLE

Serves 4

Ingredients

cracked ice

2 bananas

225 ml/8 fl oz pineapple juice,
chilled

125 ml/4 fl oz lime juice

pineapple slices, to decorate

1. Put the cracked ice into a blender. Peel the bananas and slice directly into the blender. Add the pineapple and lime juice and blend until smooth.

2. Pour into chilled glasses and dress with the slices of pineapple. Serve immediately.

MOCHA SLUSH

Serves 1

Ingredients

crushed ice cubes

100 ml/3½ fl oz coffee syrup

45 ml/3 tbsp chocolate syrup

200 ml/7 fl oz milk

grated chocolate

1. Whizz the crushed ice in a small blender with the coffee and chocolate syrups and milk until slushy.

2. Pour into a chilled glass and sprinkle with grated chocolate. Serve immediately.

MOCHA CREAM

Serves 2

Ingredients

200 ml/7 fl oz milk

50 ml/2 fl oz single cream

1 tbsp brown sugar

2 tbsp cocoa powder

1 tbsp coffee syrup or instant coffee powder

6 ice cubes

whipped cream and grated chocolate, to decorate

1. Put the milk, cream and sugar into a food processor or blender and process gently until combined.

2. Add the cocoa powder and coffee syrup and process well, then add the ice cubes and process until smooth.

3. Pour the mixture into glasses. Top with whipped cream, scatter the grated chocolate over the drinks and serve immediately.

ARNOLD PALMER

Serves 1

Ingredients

ice cubes

3 measures lemonade

3 measures iced tea

1. Half fill a chilled highball glass with ice cubes and pour in the lemonade.

2. Slowly pour in the tea, so that it does not mix.

3. Serve immediately with a straw.

Fact
This refreshing combination of iced tea and lemonade is named after American golfer Arnold Palmer.

SALTY PUPPY

Serves 1

Ingredients

granulated sugar
coarse salt
wedge of lime
cracked ice
½ measure lime juice
grapefruit juice

1. Mix equal quantities of the sugar and salt together on a saucer.

2. Rub the rim of a chilled highball glass with a wedge of lime and dip it into the sugar and salt mixture to frost.

3. Fill the glass with cracked ice and pour the lime juice over them. Top up with grapefruit juice and serve immediately.

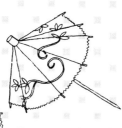

CLAM DIGGER

Serves 1

Ingredients

10-12 cracked ice cubes

hot pepper sauce

Worcestershire sauce

4 measures tomato juice

4 measures clam juice

¼ tsp horseradish sauce

celery salt and freshly ground black pepper

celery stick and wedge of lime, to decorate

1. Put 4-6 cracked ice cubes into a cocktail shaker. Dash the hot pepper sauce and Worcestershire sauce over the ice, pour in the tomato juice and clam juice and add the horseradish sauce. Shake vigorously until frosted.

2. Fill a chilled Collins glass with cracked ice cubes and strain the cocktail over them. Season to taste with celery salt and pepper and decorate with a celery stick and lime wedge. Serve immediately.

COCONUT ISLANDER

Serves 4

Ingredients

1 pineapple

4 measures pineapple juice

2 tbsp creamed coconut

4 measures milk

2 tbsp crushed pineapple

3 tbsp coconut flakes

crushed ice

cherries and pineapple leaves, to decorate

1. Cut the top off the pineapple and remove the flesh. Use some of the flesh and set aside the rest for a salad or dessert.

2. Whizz all the liquid ingredients in a blender with the coconut flakes and a little crushed ice for 30-40 seconds.

3. When smooth and frothy, pour into the pineapple shell, dress with cherries or the pineapple leaves and serve immediately with straws.

CRANBERRY PUNCH

Serves 10

Ingredients

600 ml/1 pint cranberry juice

600 ml/1 pint orange juice

150 ml/5 fl oz water

½ tsp ground ginger

¼ tsp cinnamon

¼ tsp freshly grated nutmeg

cracked ice

frozen cranberries and their leaves, to decorate

1. Put the first six ingredients into a saucepan and bring to the boil. Reduce the heat and simmer for 5 minutes.

2. Remove from the heat and pour into a heatproof jug or bowl. Chill in the refrigerator.

3. Remove from the refrigerator, put cracked ice into the serving glasses, pour in the punch, and decorate with cranberries and their leaves on cocktail sticks.

NON-ALCOHOLIC PIMM'S

Serves 6

Ingredients

600 ml/1 pint lemonade, chilled

450 ml/16 fl oz cola, chilled

450 ml/16 fl oz dry ginger ale, chilled

juice of 1 orange

juice of 1 lemon

few drops of Angostura bitters

sliced fruit and sprigs of mint

ice cubes

1. Mix the first six ingredients together thoroughly in a large jug or punch bowl.

2. Float in the fruit and mint, keep in a cold place and add the ice cubes just before serving.

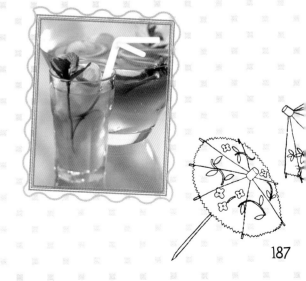

This edition published by Parragon Books Ltd in 2014
LOVE FOOD is an imprint of Parragon Books Ltd

Parragon Books Ltd
Chartist House
15–17 Trim Street
Bath BA1 1HA, UK
www.parragon.com/lovefood

Copyright © Parragon Books Ltd 2014

LOVE FOOD and the accompanying heart device is a registered trademark of Parragon Books Ltd
in Australia, the UK, USA, India and the EU.

All rights reserved. No part of this publication may be reproduced, stored in a retrieval system
or transmitted, in any form or by any means, electronic, mechanical, photocopying, recording or
otherwise, without the prior permission of the copyright holder.

ISBN: 978-1-4723-4055-9

Printed in China

New recipes by Kim Davies
New photography by Mike Cooper
Illustrations by Charlotte Farmer

Notes for the Reader
This book uses both metric and imperial measurements. Follow the same units of measurement
throughout; do not mix metric and imperial. All spoon measurements are level: teaspoons are
assumed to be 5 ml, and tablespoons are assumed to be 15 ml. Unless otherwise stated, milk is
assumed to be full fat, eggs and individual vegetables are medium, and pepper is freshly ground
black pepper.

Garnishes, decorations and serving suggestions are all optional and not necessarily included in the
recipe ingredients or method. Please consume alcohol responsibly.

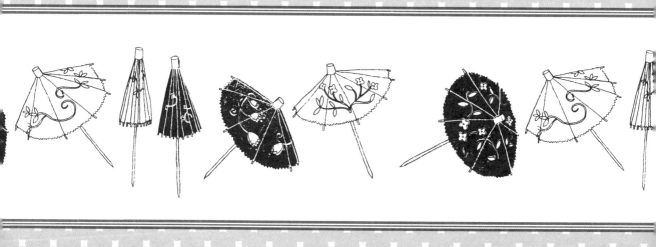